W9-ACD-442

Integrating the Literature of Beverly Cleary in the Classroom

by
Thomas J. Palumbo

illustrated by Vanessa Filkins

Cover by Vanessa Filkins

Copyright © Good Apple, 1991

ISBN No. 0-86653-610-8

Printing No. 9876

© Good Apple
A Division of Frank Schaffer Publications, Inc.
23740 Hawthorne Boulevard
Torrance, CA 90505-5927

Table of Contents

GA1329

Introduction: Author's Notes

I do not know what I may appear to the world; but to myself I seem to have been only like a boy playing on the seashore and diverting myself in now and then finding a smoother pebble or prettier shell than ordinary, whilst the great ocean of truth lay all undiscovered before me.

Brewster's Memoirs of Newton

Integrating the Literature of Beverly Cleary in the Classroom is a companion book to *Integrating the Literature of Judy Blume in the Classroom*. The *Judy Blume* introduction stressed how to build a classroom and school literature program, developing courses and workshops in children's literature, teacher training suggestions, classroom library suggestions, a unit on understanding authors and suggestions for money raising to increase the size of classroom and school libraries. *Beverly Cleary* will further refine the ten-step literature format used in *Judy Blume* and give students and teachers hundreds of additional ideas in the introduction and development of any children's literature selection, as well as the eleven Beverly Cleary books introduced in this guide.

Step One: Lead-Ins to Literature

After twenty-four years of teaching, there is no doubt in my mind that the crazier the lead-in, the greater the attention. I have dressed up as a robot, worn crazy sneakers, exploded a firecracker, made a hat out of cheese and danced (on my desk) to a Beach Boy's tune. No, I don't recommend these things to my student teachers, but I am constantly looking for those things that will compete for the attention of students caught up in the television/ad agency approach to getting viewers' attention. A lead-in has to pique the potential readers' interests and lead them into creative directions the new book may or may not take them. All teacher texts start out by introducing vocabulary . . . Boring! Boring! I know the importance of vocabulary. But once you get students interested in reading the book, then you can hit them with the drills and word development ideas and spoil the idea of a computer that takes over the mind of any student that sits behind it (William Buckley book).

If you are using the Beverly Cleary books that are contained in this book, you don't have to cover every lead-in question. Pick the ones that will generate good large and small group discussions. Change the questions' wording and add ideas of your own. Ask your students for suggestions of things they'd like to discuss or predict before beginning the story.

Step Two: Vexing Vocabulary

My two primary vocabulary goals for this section are to help students to become more understanding readers and to sharpen creative writing skills. The first way to do this is to develop vocabulary in context and the second is an endless array of writing projects and little gimmicks to show students there is only so much you can say without a wide vocabulary. The age of the computer has helped us by giving the word counts of all stories, so students can go back and change things they have used three or four times. "Words you can't use in today's writing" boxes on the right-hand side of your bulletin board listing all the forbidden words in today's writing have also been a great help. A typical box would contain the words *but, then, next, because* and *so*, while another day's forbidden words might be *big, large, small, tiny* and *to*.

Step Three: Just the Facts

There is nothing pretty about this section. There is a time in every student's life when he/she must know what fact was just presented in the story. You don't have to infer anything. Just find and support the fact. Encourage children to write the ten facts they think should be asked in the Just the Facts section. It will challenge their critical thinking skills.

Step Four: What Is Your Opinion?

This has proved to be the most enjoyable section for me. It allows everyone to give/defend/discuss his opinions on a wide range of topics included in the books that are being read, as well as issues we are confronted with every day. One of my goals is for students to see both sides of a situation. You will find that throughout this book I ask students to express their opinions and also the opinions completely opposite to their thoughts. The results have been outstanding. Very rarely now are my classes completely for one point of view on an issue.

Step Five: Ideas and Illustrations

Literature has to be integrated into all the curriculums to be successful. Art seems to be the natural starting point. Even if you think you can't draw or if you don't have ideas of your own, you can still pattern yourself after the great masters. Try to understand and pick up some of their techniques and patterns. Quiz yourself as to why an illustrator decided to draw what he did. Suggest illustrations for pages that don't have any. We have cut so many great paintings in half to re-create the other half that the art museum will soon be coming after us for distorting the minds of children. Illustrate everything you do with drawings or creative uses of cutout pictures. Place illustrations on the essays you compose for the subjects.

Step Six: Drills for Skills

Like all teachers, I am always looking for ways to make knowledge stick on sometimes very slippery brains. This book and the other six I have written contain over five hundred multilevel, easily adaptable ideas for skill development. The spur-of-the-moment ideas always seem to be better than the things that take me hours to write and draw. My favorite in this category is creating literature crosses. A large improvement on test scores can be attributed to this silly little idea. A word cross is formed when you take a vocabulary word and cross it at a common letter with a word that has the same meaning. A child cannot cross *tiny* with the word *small* because they do not have any letters in common. This forces the writer to expand his/her vocabulary skills and look for another word like *little* that will cross the original. However, to stimulate original creative thinking, another wrinkle is added. The "word crosser" is to try to think of a word cross that no one else on his/her team has chosen. *Tiny* might be crossed by *minute* (watch your pronunciation) to create a winning entry.

Step Seven: Short-Term Projects

Teachers constantly tell me that they do not have enough time in the day for student projects. In this book I have tried to assure that every piece of the reading, math and social studies curricula is integrated into the Short-Term Project, Teacher Suggestions and Research Suggestions sections. Student creativity, excitement and self-direction through the use of these projects always end in advance student knowledge and self-worth. Because of the fantastic results you see by using a few of the projects in this book, you will find that project time is time well spent. Books can take you all sorts of places. I tried to make some selections directly related to the stories, while others will hopefully take you and your students far afield of the original ideas.

Step Ten: Write Like a Master

This is a new section that wasn't included in my *Judy Blume* book. My school district is big on sustained silent reading and sustained silent writing. I found that my kids needed more direction than just "write on anything for fifteen minues." Every day I racked my brain for new writing ideas. I started by giving my classes half a paragraph from a famous writer and then they completed the rest. They were Kurt Vonnegut one day and Robert Nathan the next. Then I went to original story starters. It was like pulling teeth in the beginning, because everyone wanted to know how many words or sentences he had to write before I'd accept the final draft. Everyone, also, had to read my part of the story as he read his "continuation" to the class. By the end of the year, the shop-till-you-drop phone conversation and murder mysteries seemed to all be written by professionals. My most reluctant writer, at the end of the year, told me that "I should think of writing a book of stories like the ones we do in class every day." I immediately changed her final grade of a C to a B. It is my hope that your C's will be changed to A's and B's after using the Judy Blume/Beverly Cleary series.

1 · 2 · 3 · 4 · 5 · 6 · 7 · 8 · 9 · 10

GA1329

What Makes a Successful Author

Beverly Cleary has been writing children's books for over thirty years. She is read by millions of children all over the world. Her books have made us appreciate and respect the art of writing and, at the same time, respect those around us. Through the magic of her writing, she has taken us from the small world of Ralph S. Mouse to the difficult world of first dates. We have visited behind grandfather's clock, gone to the Maclane wedding and studied in California. She has helped us understand friendship, love, caring, common sense, difficult situations, happiness, grown-ups and growing up. She has made us realize that most of our problems have been experienced by others and, just like her characters, we can find solutions to many of them.

This could have been the brief description of Beverly Cleary that appeared on any number of her book covers. It makes us think and see the scope of her writing, but it really doesn't tell us any real information about Beverly Cleary. Who, then, is Beverly Cleary? Maybe some of these questions will allow you to look at Beverly Cleary, the person, a little more closely. Maybe you will use some of these same questions to examine the authors of other books that you have read.

1. What do you think Beverly Cleary's childhood was like?

2. Who do you think she based Henry Huggins, Ramona, Beezus and her other characters on?

3. Do you think her childhood was a happy one?

4. How much of her own pets do you think she reflects in each of her writings of Ralph S. Mouse and Ribsy?

5. Why has she been so successful writing for young children and older children as well?

6. What writers and storytellers do you think influenced her writings and life?

7. Where can we go to get some solid inside information about her?

8. What other authors would you compare to her? How did you make this determination? Are her stories like Judy Blume's or are they quite different?

9. Do you think the things that Beverly Cleary writes about could have happened thirty years ago? Thirty years from now? Can a good story be put in any time frame?

GA1329

Ramona and Her Father

Lost Job

Walking on Stilts

Bleating Sheep

Television Jingles

No Smoking Campaign

2

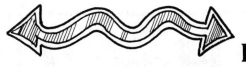

Lead-Ins to Literature

What would you do if one or both of your parents were out of work? Would you try to make their lives easier or would you go on a campaign to make them stop smoking? Would you put No Smoking signs all over the place or would you just try to behave, so your parents can worry about where the next dollar is coming from, instead of worrying about you? Ramona is in a similar situation . . . and more!

1. Is there anyone in your family that smokes? How do you feel about them smoking?

   _____

2. What type of events do you think would be in a father/daughter story? Do you think the situations would be any different if it were mother/daughter or mother/son? Which one of these choices would have the most interest or would sell the most books?

   _____

3. If you did not see the cover of this book, what type of illustrations would you predict that the illustrator would use on the cover to attract the reader's attention?

   _____

4. Would you make the father in a father/daughter story a strong character or one with lots of troubles? Would you set up situations where he helps his daughter or ones where the daughter is a great help to the dad? Please explain why you chose "Dad Helps Daughter" or "Daughter Helps Dad." Survey your class to see which type of plot your classmates preferred.

   _____

5. What type of troubles might the daughter start with older brothers and sisters that would annoy her parents?

   _____

6. How old would you make the daughter in a story like this? How would the daughter's age change the plot and setting? Try to let your mind see the daughter in at least three different stages, each about five years apart.

   _____

7. What is the strangest job that you'd give the father in your story? Write your five best choices on a piece of paper. Select in your mind the one that you think is the strangest/most original before giving the paper to a friend. Have your friend select his favorite and see if your choices match.

   _____

8. Beverly Cleary grew up in Portland, Oregon. How might this affect the ideas she uses in her stories? Do you think it will have an effect on the father's character in this story?

   _____

9. If you were making a movie, what movie star would you pick for the daughter? The father? Why? Please explain.

   _____

10. What books have you read that would make good Father's Day presents? Mother's Day? Why? See how this story compares to your choices.

    _____

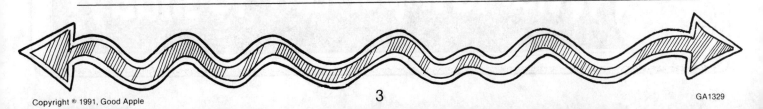

GA1329

Vexing Vocabulary I
Student Generated

One of the hardest jobs a teacher has is teaching his/her students to make their own decisions on what is important to study. Instead of studying things you already know, this work sheet will give you a chance to generate words that you don't know. Words that you think are special or words that you would like to remember should also be recorded below.

What two words would you pick from *Ramona and Her Father* to study in each of the following categories?

1. Person's name _____ _____

2. A place _____ _____

3. A noun _____ _____

4. An adjective _____ _____

5. A compound word _____ _____

6. A scientific word _____ _____

7. A foreign word or word generated from another language_____ _____

8. A well-written phrase _____

   _____

9. A hard-to-spell word _____ _____

10. A commonly confused word_____ _____

Select ten words from the story that would add to your writing skills. You are a TV host of a program called *Father and Daughter*. Use the ten words in your description of the program.

_____ _____ _____ _____ _____

_____ _____ _____ _____ _____

Show host's name _____ Assistant's name _____

_____

_____

_____

_____

_____

What is important to study?

GA1329

Vexing Vocabulary II

guided	whetstones	impatient
dainty	camera	moistened
conspicuous	hazardous	cigarettes
shivery	congregation	margarine
faucet	jagged	scarcely
ferocious	voice	Olympics
checker	bleated	bur
coziness	silence	tangled

Place the correct vocabulary words in the blanks below. The first sentences are made easier for you because the first letter of the answer is given. The last ten sentences may contain more than one correct answer.

1. Smoking may be h _____ to your health.

2. The s_____ was eerie.

3. The singer's v _____ cracked.

4. She was cut by a j _____ piece of glass.

5. The c _____ made two mistakes on our bill.

6. "I'll be right there. Don't be so i _____!"

7. The horse had a b _____ under its saddlecloth.

8. Did you put m_____ or butter on your corn?

9. What do you know about g_____ missiles?

10. The minister spoke to his c_____.

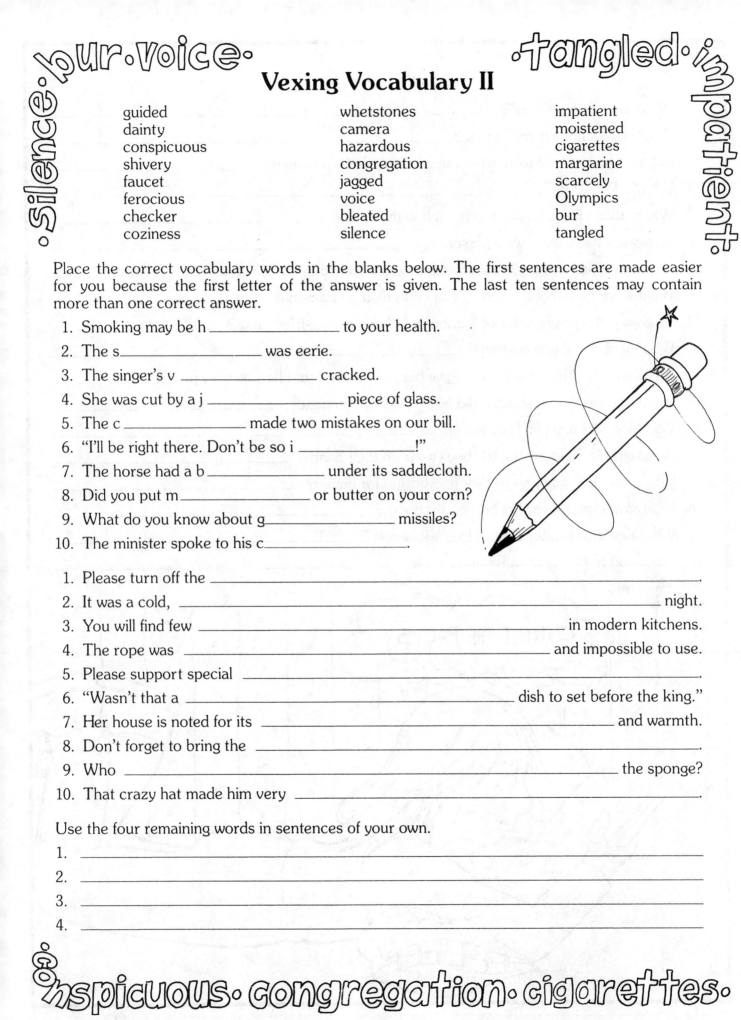

1. Please turn off the _____.

2. It was a cold, _____ night.

3. You will find few _____ in modern kitchens.

4. The rope was _____ and impossible to use.

5. Please support special _____.

6. "Wasn't that a _____ dish to set before the king."

7. Her house is noted for its _____ and warmth.

8. Don't forget to bring the _____.

9. Who _____ the sponge?

10. That crazy hat made him very _____.

Use the four remaining words in sentences of your own.

1. _____

2. _____

3. _____

4. _____

5

GA1329

Just the Facts

1. What are "Tommy-Toes"? _____

2. What did Ramona name her cat? _____

3. In Mrs. Quimby's opinion, what ate up the Quimby's money? _____

4. What is Puss-Puddy? _____

5. Where didn't Ramona want to be "left with her awe"? _____

6. Why were there three wise persons? _____

7. How many years younger than Ramona was the child in the television commercial? _____

8. What color Gummybear had its head bitten off by Ramona? _____

9. What was the future color of Ramona's father's smoke-filled lungs? _____

10. Who needed a sheep costume? _____

11. What signal did Ramona's father give her to show her that he was very proud of her? _____

12. What two pieces of the outfit did Mrs. Quimby complete? _____

13. Was Mrs. Quimby good at sewing? _____

14. What did Mr. Russo make the boys wear on their heads? _____

15. Why didn't the family go to Whopperburger for dinner? _____

16. Who didn't want a spoiled brat on his hands? _____

17. What did Ramona describe as the "wickedest"? _____

18. What had to be cut from Ramona's hair? _____

JUST THE FACTS

GA1329

What Is Your Opinion?

1. Do you think Ramona's antismoking campaign was overdone? Could it have been handled differently? How would you have gone about changing your parents' smoking habits?

_____

_____

2. Is it possible that even the cat was grumpy while Ramona's dad was out of work? _____

3. Can animals tell the difference between more expensive and cheaper food? How? Why not?

_____

_____

4. In your opinion what are the three best TV jingles? Record your answers and compare them to your classmates'. Do jingles appeal more to children or adults? Explain.

_____

_____

5. Is it possible for someone to try too hard to make someone happy? _____

_____

6. Would you choose Halloween as the best "dress up day" or are there other choices that would be just as much fun? What other choices would qualify for this "best dressed up day" list? _____

_____

7. What is the worst thing about being out of work? _____

8. Do you think that the author could have chosen a more appropriate song than "Ninety-Nine Bottles of Beer" for a young child like Ramona to sing? _____

9. This is a Newbery Award book. Why do you think it was given this outstanding award?

_____

_____

10. Are kindergartners cute and second graders ignored in your school, also? Would you call the lines in your school straight or wobbly? _____

_____

11. Teachers are always telling students to be creative. What does this mean? Is creativity any different in writing, speaking or mathematics? What can you do to make your answers to these questions more creative? _____

_____

12. Beezus twirls to be inspired. What is the best way to be inspired? Collect four answers from people out of your classroom and share them with your classmates and teacher. What four ways do you use to be inspired? Compare lists. _____

_____

13. Ramona listened to her parents' discussion through the furnace grate. What comments do you have about this? _____

_____

14. What is the funniest thing one of your pets ate or tried to eat? Compile a class list of items. _____

_____

15. What is the worst thing about creative writing? _____

_____

Ideas and Illustrations

An illustration plate contains three scenes in chronological or story order. Cartoonists usually have three or four scenes on their plates. Review the comic strips in your local newspaper or the Sunday paper before designing your own plates using the themes below. Two illustration plates are provided for you below. You can use them for planning and classmate/teacher input before enlarging your ideas on 11" x 14" (27.94 x 35.56 cm) paper. After working with some of the ideas suggested, design a mini story format of your own. Combine your writing talents with a classmate's drawing talents to form a team effort original illustration plate.

Illustration Plate Theme Ideas

A dog and a cat fighting   A mother designing a new outfit
Ramona drawing smoking posters   Baby standing in crib
A scene from a school play   Child eating ice cream
Fancy smoke rings circling smoker's head   Child flying kite
Christmas tree being decorated   Phone booth usage
Child sleeping with teddy bear   Kids walking on stilt cans

Theme:

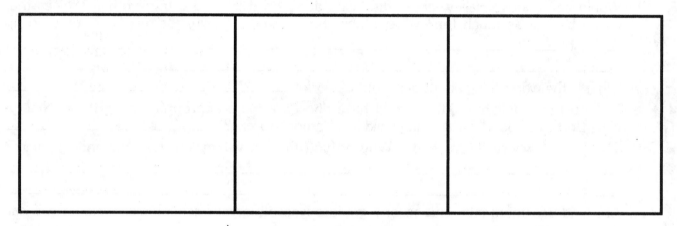

Theme:

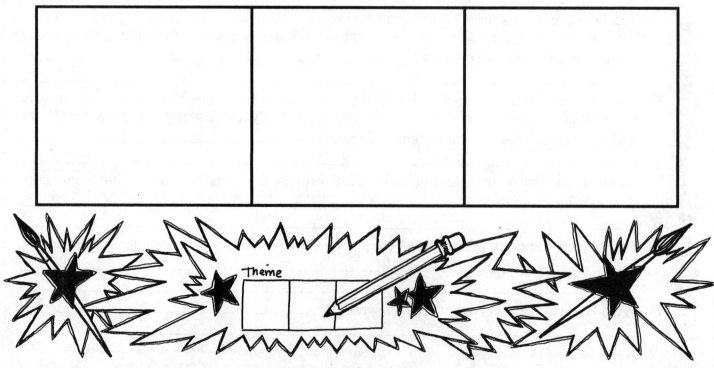

GA1329

Famous Wise People of Fact and Fiction
Short-Term Project

Name_____ Date_____

Famous Wise People of Fact and Fiction focuses on those people who have used exceptional wisdom in the quest for a better life, justice, knowledge and solutions to the age-old problems of mankind. You are to research two people in the fact area and two people in the fiction area of this topic. Your information should contain your sources and illustrations, graphs or charts.

Some suggested topics might involve research about:

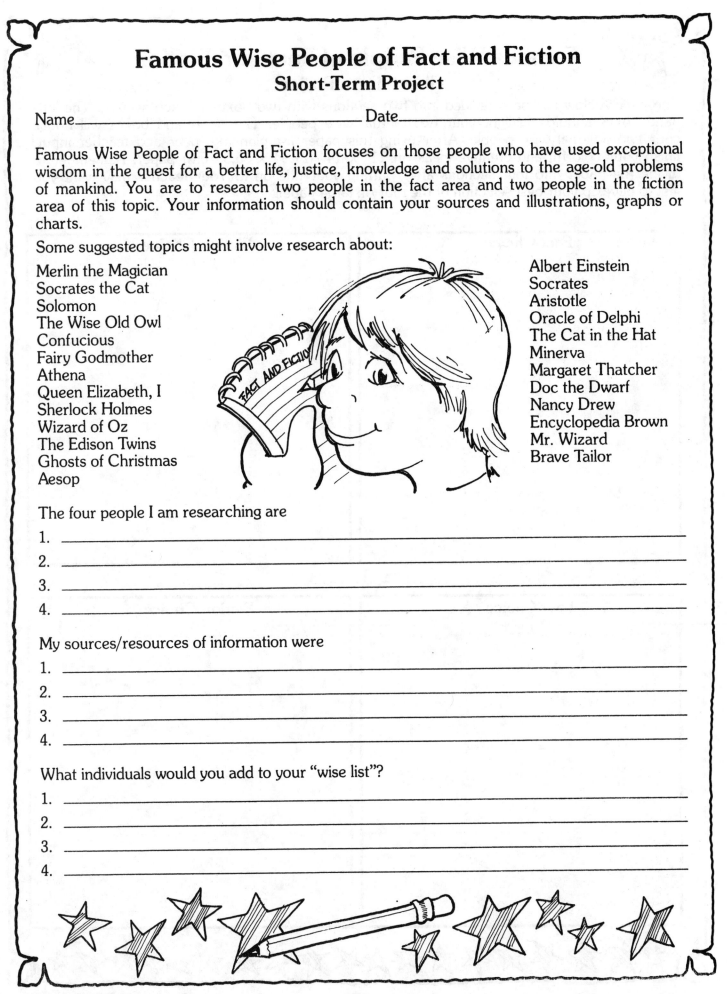

Merlin the Magician
Socrates the Cat
Solomon
The Wise Old Owl
Confucious
Fairy Godmother
Athena
Queen Elizabeth, I
Sherlock Holmes
Wizard of Oz
The Edison Twins
Ghosts of Christmas
Aesop

Albert Einstein
Socrates
Aristotle
Oracle of Delphi
The Cat in the Hat
Minerva
Margaret Thatcher
Doc the Dwarf
Nancy Drew
Encyclopedia Brown
Mr. Wizard
Brave Tailor

The four people I am researching are

1. _____
2. _____
3. _____
4. _____

My sources/resources of information were

1. _____
2. _____
3. _____
4. _____

What individuals would you add to your "wise list"?

1. _____
2. _____
3. _____
4. _____

GA1329

Famous Wise People of Fact and Fiction
Short-Term Project

The paper below has been divided into two sections with two boxes in each section. The left-hand boxes should highlight your two factual wise people. The right-hand boxes will house your two fictional wise people. After using this paper for planning, peer and teacher input, finish your colorful and creative ideas on 11″ x 14″ (27.94 x 35.56 cm) paper. Remember to divide the paper into four sections after putting your title on it. Your teacher may want you just to develop your best selection of the four on large paper.

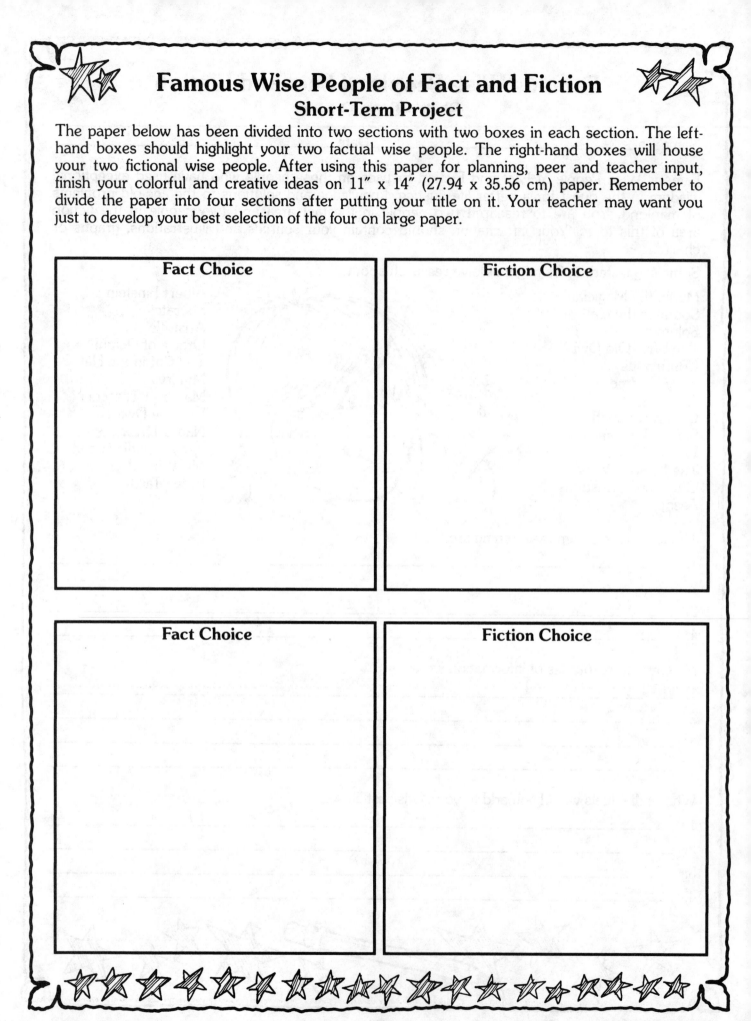

Fact Choice

Fiction Choice

Fact Choice

Fiction Choice

Proverbs/Wisdom
Short-Term Project

After researching well-known proverbs and words of wisdom, pick two and explain them to your classmates. Record ten of your favorites and illustrate four of them. Pick four proverbs from the list below to illustrate in the spaces provided, or use 11″ x 14″ (27.94 x 35.56 cm) paper to enlarge your ideas.

1. What goes up must come down
2. Get mad, get glad
3. Where there is a will, there's a way
4. Like father, like son
5. Too many cooks spoil the broth
6. A penny saved is a penny earned
7. No news is good news
8. Early to bed early to rise, makes a man healthy, wealthy and wise
9. A rolling stone gathers no moss
10. Each to his own taste
11. Better late than never
12. A soft answer turns away anger

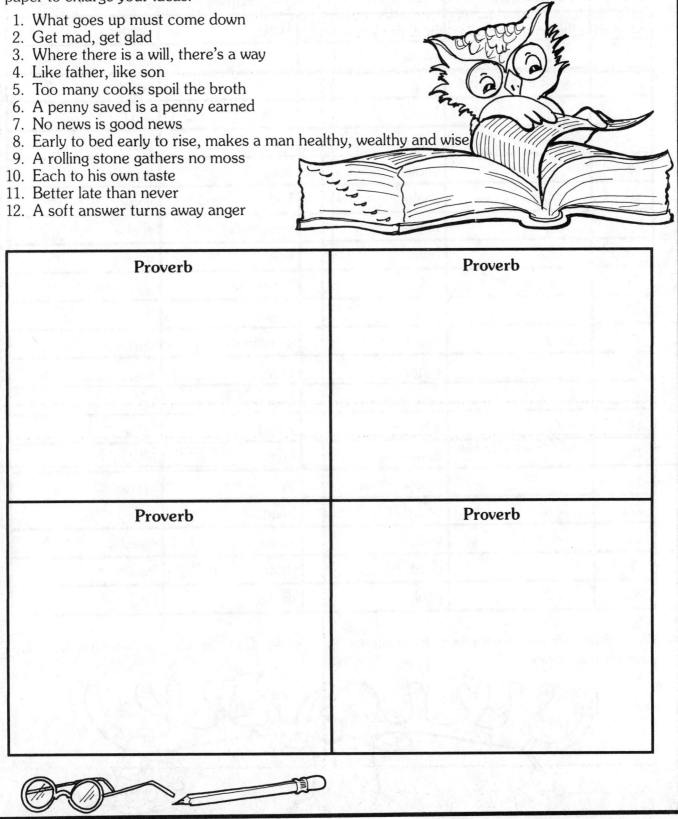

Proverb	**Proverb**
Proverb	**Proverb**

GA1329

Triple Play Words
Drills for Skills

Each of the three words listed across have one word in common. When you find that word you have completed a triple play. See how many triple plays you can solve in the list below.

Key	Word	Triples		
Ex.	big	foot	Ben	dipper
1.		white	man	ball
2.		bean	jacks	rope
3.		horse	shell	port
4.		cream	berg	pick
5.		shovel	boat	engine
6.		shake	ball	some
7.		man	chocolate	shake
8.		body	one	where
9.		old soul	Christmas	go round
10.		ache	stand	line
11.		side	standing	come
12.		room	time	bug
13.		coat	broken	fly
14.		tub	room	robe
15.		house	bulb	weight
16.		side	to	come
17.		board	head	time
18.		walk	show	effects
19.		giant	thumb	beans
20.		pool	dealer	lot

Write three triples of your own to challenge your class. Use the blank master on the next page for your work.

GA1329

Triple Play Words
Drills for Skills—Blank Master

Each of the three words listed across have one word in common. When you find that word you have completed a triple play. Make up your own triple plays below.

Key	Word	Triples		
Ex.	big	foot	Ben	dipper
1.				
2.				
3.				
4.				
5.				
6.				
7.				
8.				
9.				
10.				
11.				
12.				
13.				
14.				
15.				
16.				
17.				
18.				
19.				
20.				

Exchange this sheet with a friend.

GA1329

Research Suggestions

1. Research smoking regulations in your school, town and state. Did you find any significant differences among the three choices?

2. Find out what percentage of men and women smoke nationally and compare these figures with the mothers and fathers of children in your classroom. Are there more mothers or fathers that smoke? Make a chart showing how many mothers and fathers smoke now . . . in three months . . . in six months . . . by the end of the school year.

3. Find out why people smoke and give a speech offering "better choices for smokers."

4. Of the people who quit smoking, do more people do it on their own or with help from outside the family sources? Interview ten people who have quit and find out how they did it. Combine your list with your classmates', and see if you can reach any conclusions. Make a profile of what the person who was able to quit smoking is like.

5. Make a graph of children in your class and the animals that they have dressed up like in either a school play, Halloween or any other occasion.

6. Interview someone else's mom on what other "money burners" they would add to Mrs. Quimby's list in addition to taxes, groceries and house payments/rent.

7. Find out what the three top brands of cat foods are. Survey your classmates that have cats. Find out how many use the top three brands. Find out how many feed their cats dry cat food or cat food from a can. Do a similar study of kitty litter favorites.

8. Design a Top Pet of the Year Award. List the criteria for the award, and then highlight the reasons your pet or a TV/movie pet is your choice for the honor. Place your pet selection on a colorful poster. Display the choices/posters of your classmates on a classroom clothesline.

9. Mrs. Quimby wasn't wild about sewing Ramona's costume. List the ten things that parents do for their children of all ages that they aren't wild about. Certainly changing diapers should be first on everyone's list.

10. What three plays would you like your classroom to perform? What parts/jobs would you play in each selection?

11. Take a survey of things most commonly caught in people's hair and then collect "weird hair happenings."

12. Make up and research ten "believe it or not" questions for your classmates. Score ten points for each one answered incorrectly.

GA1329

Teacher Suggestions

1. Research with your class the number of products and sayings that are characterized with the words *smart, wise* or any other wisdom-related analogy.

Products	**Sayings**
Wise potato chips	smarty-cat
prodigy	birdbrain
salt free pretzels	wise guy

2. Have a member of your local health service agency present "the real medical facts" about smoking. Our local police station provides a cigarette, alcohol and drug avoidance training person as a regular part of each of our classroom (k-8) programs. Maybe you can develop such a program at your school.

3. Have an Animals from Literature Dress-up Day and luncheon. Each child gives a mini view of his character's significance to the overall story in which he appears. Each luncheon place mat is the cover representation of the story. Newspapers are happy to cover this event.

4. Discuss job qualifications with your class. Each student will then pick an occupation and create a job scenario. Have students design posters listing the skills that they have exhibited on their imaginary jobs and at the same time ask to be promoted to new jobs.

5. Play Chalkboard Jeopardy with categories from literature as your topics. Some topics might be transportation, animals, lead characters, fairy tales, myths and legends, and nursery rhymes. Write the questions on 3" x 5" (7.62 x 12.7 cm) cards. Put the categories on the board with $10, $20, $30, $40 and $50 under them. Each time a category price is selected, erase its value. Divide the class in half and keep a running score.

6. What kind of support services are available in your town that are similar to the Big Brother, Big Sister program. Their representatives, like the Police Athletic League, are always anxious to talk to children. It doesn't matter whether you have or don't have a predominant amount of single parent children. It's just nice for children to know about other opinions.

7. Check your local library for a list of oral storytellers in your area. The children appreciate listening to someone in addition to the teacher. Local librarians love to give "book talks" to children and sign them up for library cards at the same time.

8. Have your children write "cute" letters to their favorite authors asking them to come to school to read to the class and talk about their books. Luck and circumstances sometimes run together.

9. Write the National Cancer Society for information that they provide to schools.

Research
Discuss
Play
Support
Write

15

Write Like a Master

Complete the three story starters below using the theme of a character who is constantly getting into trouble. Some of the trouble is on purpose, but most of it can't be helped. Try to use some of the story's vocabulary words as you creatively finish each starter.

Story Starter I

Crash! That is the third lamp I've broken this week. Mom is going to put me behind bars for the rest of my life. The first two were just cheap lamps, but this one has been her favorite for years. She said her mother gave it to her before she died, and each time she sees it burning brightly in the window when she comes home . . . well, you know. This cast on my foot keeps making me lose my balance. It seems that every time I begin to fall I grab _____

_____

_____

_____

_____

Story Starter II

There is no way to describe the mayhem that Bruce and Betty caused. How can a kitten and a puppy do so much damage? Their previous owner told us they were both frisky. This mess adds a new dimension to the word *frisky*. Fifteen unwatched minutes of frisky isn't a long time in my book. Just look at the living room. There isn't a single _____

_____

_____

_____

_____

Story Starter III

I honestly made every attempt to get through the day without getting into any trouble. Sometimes that is extremely difficult to do, even when you are really trying your best. Trouble seems to follow me around like a shadow on a bright day. Trouble must have thought of me as his friend. He would quietly call me over to discuss some can't-miss opportunities of the day. These opportunities would stand your hair on end. I should have known by now how not to listen to him. Maybe I should enroll in one of those antitrouble training courses . . . you know one of the courses where _____

_____

_____

_____

_____

GA1329

The Ramona Quimby Diary

Special Occasions

RAMONA AND BEEZUS KEEP OUT OF MY DIARY

Dear Diary

Rainy Day Thoughts

Hot Stickers

RAMONA THE BRAT

RAMONA, AGE 8

RAMONA THE PEST

RAMONA AND HER FATHER

Mom's Diary

Misspelled Words

GA1329

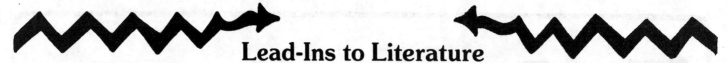

Lead-Ins to Literature

Did you ever think you would like to be two places at the same time? Have you ever wished you could jump into a book or movie and be one of the characters? Did you ever wish that your personal journal or diary was a little more exciting? *The Ramona Quimby Diary* lets you do all three. Of course, you must have the ability to change characters at the flip of a page.

1. When you heard the title *The Ramona Quimby Diary*, did you think you were going to read Ramona's personal thoughts and daily entries about her childhood?

   _____

   _____

2. Have you read any Ramona books or watched her PBS series on TV? Which books did you like the most? Which TV episodes came closest to the books that you have read? Were any of the TV episodes completely different from the books?

   _____

   _____

3. The Beverly Cleary books I have read are

   _____

   _____

4. What famous diaries have you talked about in class or read at home? Does anyone in your family keep a diary?

   _____

   _____

5. All ship commanders and *Star Trek* captains must keep logs. How would you predict *The Ramona Quimby Diary* might be similar or might be different from their writings?

   Similar

   _____

   _____

   Different

   _____

   _____

6. What kind of binder do you picture when someone mentions he has an old diary? Do you picture the jeweled encasements of a king in the Middle Ages or a group of daily jottings tied together with a favorite bow or ribbon?

   _____

   _____

7. Can you name three good secret hiding places for your diary? Don't worry, I won't tell! No way! Honest!

   _____

   _____

GA1329

Fractional Vocabulary Words

Vexing Vocabulary

investigated	linen	faucet
glee	hilarious	turnips
mosquito	faint	initial
personal	curdled	humdrum
Chiquita	crouched	engagement
valentine	dandelion	familiar
crayons	perfume	situation
impatience	behave	glimpse

A fractional vocabulary word is a word that has a smaller word of three or more letters in it. One and two-letter words within a larger word are not accepted for this activity. Three blanks are provided for you. Place the original word in blank one. In blank two, place the smaller word contained in the original. Some originals have more than one word hidden in them. Try to select the smaller word with the most letters. In blank three you will form a fraction by placing the number of letters in the smaller word over the number of letters in the original. Try to remember the smaller words in the original when it comes to spelling test time. This activity is designed to help make you a better speller.

	Original	Hidden Word	Fraction
1.	investigated	invest	$\frac{6}{12} = \frac{1}{2}$
2.			
3.			
4.			
5.			
6.			
7.			
8.			
9.			
10.			
11.			
12.			
13.			
14.			
15.			

Try doing this with the names of children in your class.

16.			
17.			

19

GA1329

Just the Facts

1. What did the girls find hilarious in Mrs. Quimby's diary? _____

2. What letters did Mrs. Quimby mess up? _____

3. How did the girls start their diaries? _____

4. In what book did Ramona talk about her "curdled niceness"? _____

5. In *Ramona Forever* what did Ramona wear plastered to her forehead? _____

6. Ramona stated, "I've got an engagement ring, and I'm going to marry you." Who was the object of her affections? _____

7. What did Ramona do to Susan's owl in *Ramona the Brave*? _____

8. What kind of stilts did Ramona and Howie build in the book *Ramona and Her Father*? _____

9. Beezus had her feelings hurt when Ramona called her _____ instead of Pieface?

10. What type of bear did Ramona take to bed with her? _____

11. What enormous purple colored letters did Ramona put in every page of her book? _____

12. What figures did Ramona make with her Fourth of July sparkler? _____

13. What time of the year did Ramona think was long and boring? _____

14. What teacher was featured in the Book Nook? _____

15. What did Ramona like the best next to Christmas and her birthday? _____

16. When Beezus was standing next to the TV, her teased and sprayed hair looked like that of a _____ year old.

17. What does the slang word *egghead* mean? _____

GA1329

What Is Your Opinion?

1. Do you think everyone should keep a diary to record his personal thoughts and insights into the things that are happening around him?

_____

_____

2. Are most diaries written to be private or to be thoughts that can be shared years later like Mrs. Quimby did with Beezus and Ramona?

_____

_____

3. What do you think can be learned from looking at what you wrote a week ago? Month ago? Year ago? Ten years ago?

_____

_____

4. Which of the books that were included in the *Quimby Diary* did you enjoy the most? The least?

_____

_____

5. What was your opinion of the projects the author had you complete between each diary entry? Which ones did you like? How would you improve one of the projects you didn't like?

_____

_____

6. Ramona included the terrible things that she did in her diary. What characters from literature should also include the terrible things they did as entries in their diaries? What should Cinderella's stepsisters, King Henry VIII, the Coyote, Elmer Fudd, the wolf in "Peter and the Wolf," the sheriff of Nottingham or the giant in "Jack and the Beanstalk" have written?

_____

_____

7. Where and when is the best place and time to write in a diary? Is it necessary to write every day or only when recordable things happen to you?

_____

_____

8. What was the most unusual location that you used to write in your diary? If you don't have a diary, where is the most unusual place that you ever completed your homework or letter writing?

_____

_____

9. Do you think putting a Keep-Out-Ramona/Beezus sign in a diary is enough to stop someone from being nosy?

_____

_____

10. What do you think writing in a diary will teach you about yourself?

_____

_____

GA1329

Creative Page Markers
Ideas and Illustrations

The Ramona Quimby Diary has a page of specially designed stickers to mark special entries in the diary. Most people, who keep diaries, put little drawings or doodles in the upper right corner of important event pages. What illustration would you draw or what sticker would you design to place at the top of your diary for each of these months? Practice drawing two or three for each month. Place the best drawing for each month in the spaces below. Place your best drawing of all on an 8½" x 11" (21.57 x 27.94 cm) piece of paper. Have your teacher place each of your classmates' drawings and the months they represent on a clothesline in front of your windows.

January	February	March

April	May	June

July	August	September

October	November	December

GA1329

Creative Events Markers
Ideas and Illustrations

The Ramona Quimby Diary has pages of specially designed drawings and projects to mark special holidays and events in the diary. Most people, who keep diaries, put little drawings or doodles in the upper right corner of important days like New Year's, birthdays or graduation. What illustration would you draw or what sticker would you design to place at the top of your diary for each of these special events? Practice drawing two or three ideas for each situation. Place the best drawing for each event in the space below. Place your best drawing of all on an 8½″ x 11″ (21.57 x 27.94 cm) piece of paper. Have your teacher place your classmates' best drawings and the holidays or situations they represent on a clothesline in the back of your room.

New Year's Eve	Your Birthday	Your Graduation
A Baby's Birth	Halloween	Groundhog Day
April Fool's Day	A New Bike/Car	100% on an Exam
Mother's Day	Father's Day	Last Day of School

Diary Selections of Famous People in Fact and Fiction
Short-Term Project

After reading *The Ramona Quimby Diary*, keeping diary notes about yourself and discussing other famous diary writers, such as Anne Frank, in your classroom, you should be ready for this short-term project challenge. It is called Diary Selections of Famous People in Fact and Fiction. In this challenge you will choose a situation from those listed below and assume the identity of the famous person involved. You will try to write his/her exact feelings before or after an historic or not so historic event. Four lines are provided for each of your entries. Please do not let the lines confine your thoughts. Try selecting a different situation each day, or with your teacher's approval make up some of your own.

What would the diary entries look like in the following situations?

1. The entry of Sally Ride, the astronaut, the night before her first space flight

_____

_____

_____

_____

2. Sally Ride's entry her first night in space

_____

_____

_____

_____

3. Joan of Arc's thoughts before she was to be burned at the stake

_____

_____

_____

_____

4. Harriet Tubman's entry during one of her slave rescue trips

_____

_____

_____

_____

5. Columbus' entry after months on the high seas without sighting land

_____

_____

_____

_____

GA1329

6. Abraham Lincoln's entry the night before he was to present his Gettysburg Address

_____

_____

_____

7. The Wright Brothers first thought the night they found they had a vehicle that was capable of flying

_____

_____

_____

8. Frank Lloyd Wright's diary notes as his first architectural plans are being brought to life in a new building

_____

_____

_____

9. Cinderella's entry the night she learned she couldn't go to the Prince's ball

_____

_____

_____

10. Paul Lawrence Dunbar's entry the night he saw his first poem in print

_____

_____

_____

11. Robin Hood's journal evaluation the first time he met Little John and his new band of merry men

_____

_____

_____

12. Rumpelstiltskin's journal thoughts the night he thought he would definitely keep the baby

_____

_____

_____

GA1329

13. Amos Mouse's entry the first evening in Benjamin Franklin's house

_____

_____

_____

14. Betsy Ross' entry the night she was told that her flag would be used as the nation's banner

_____

_____

_____

15. Sleepy (the Dwarf) on how he feels about Grumpy always complaining

_____

_____

_____

16. Daniel Boone's entry the first night alone in the woods

_____

_____

_____

17. Snow White's diary notes the day she awakened from her sleep

_____

_____

_____

18. Robinson Crusoe after first sighting footsteps on his island

_____

_____

_____

19. George Washington's entry the last night of his horrible winter stay at Valley Forge

_____

_____

_____

20. Paul Bunyan on learning that his footsteps made the Great Lakes

_____

_____

_____

GA1329

21. Merlin the Magician's entry on learning he was responsible for young, future King Arthur's upbringing

_____
_____
_____
_____

22. Bambi's journal thoughts the night she almost lost her mother

_____
_____
_____
_____

23. Donald Duck's entry the first day that Huey went to school

_____
_____
_____
_____

24. Charles Lindbergh's airplane log halfway across the Atlantic on his first transatlantic flight

_____
_____
_____
_____

25. Icarus after his wings to freedom were constructed but not yet into motion

_____
_____
_____
_____

26. What would Sherlock Holmes write in his journal the night he solved his first case?

_____
_____
_____
_____

27. Martin Luther King's thoughts the night before his "I have a dream" speech

_____
_____
_____
_____

28. President Nixon's journal thoughts after being the first President removed from office

_____
_____
_____
_____

GA1329

29. Isaac Newton's journal entry after first discovering the laws of gravity

_____

_____

_____

30. Leonardo da Vinci's writing and next drawings after completing (what about the missing eyebrow) the Mona Lisa

_____

_____

_____

31. What would Shakespeare have written the night his first play received a standing ovation?

_____

_____

_____

32. How would Gelsey Kirkland (ballerina) have composed her diary thoughts after first dancing the lead in _Swan Lake_?

_____

_____

_____

_____

33. Can you put Neil Armstrong's diary moon scratches into some readable form?

_____

_____

_____

34. How tragic would the log of the captain of the _Titanic_ have been as he realized that rescue ships were too far away to assist his quickly sinking luxury liner?

_____

_____

_____

35. What would the tortoise have said the night after he lost that important race to the hare?

_____

_____

_____

Dear Diary

GA1329

The Multiple Word and Sentence Generator
Drills for Skills—Student Sheet

The Multiple Word and Sentence Generator is partially guaranteed to put spice, zest and uniqueness in your vocabulary. There are boxes under key words in each sentence. Place four words that are synonyms under each key word. Try to pick words that have more meaning, power and spice than the original. Color in your best choice of the four. Now read your new sentence using each colored-in word in place of the key word. You can use a thesaurus. Hopefully, your sentence now is award-winning and spicy.

Ex. The old house was near the corner.

ancient	mansion		close to		intersection
run down	shack		approximate to		turn
decrepit	home		next to		street's edge
aged	estate		touching		street's end

Please complete the sentence generators below and read the best ones to your classmates.

1. A big car raced into the night.

2. Our dear daughter is sick.

3. Don't drop that soup dish.

4. The gun was pointed at my head.

5. Her award winning song pleased my ears.

Can you design three sentence generators of your own?

GA1329

The Multiple Word and Sentence Generator
Drills for Skills—Blank Master

The Multiple Word and Sentence Generator is partially guaranteed to put spice, zest and uniqueness in your vocabulary. Your teacher will read five sentences to you. Key words in each sentence will land above the boxes. Place four words that are synonyms under each key word. Try to pick words that have more meaning, power and spice than the original. Color in your best choice of the four. Now read your new sentence using each colored-in word in place of the key word. You can use a thesaurus. Hopefully, your sentence now is award-winning and spicy.

Ex.　　The　　　old　　　house　　　was　　　near　　　the　　　corner.

ancient	mansion		close to	intersection
run down	shack		approximate to	turn
decrepit	home		next to	street's edge
aged	estate		touching	street's end

Please complete the sentence generators below and read your best ones to your classmates.

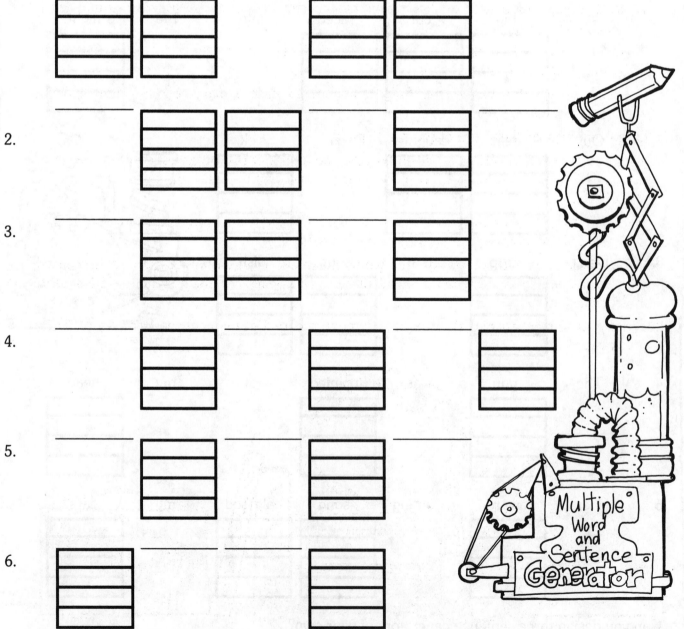

1.

2.

3.

4.

5.

6.

GA1329

Research Suggestions

1. Collect three stories of your mother's, grandmother's, aunt's or older sister's childhood to share with your class the same way Mrs. Quimby shared her diary stories with Ramona and Beezus.

2. Research the percentage of boys, girls, mothers and fathers who keep or, at one time, have recorded thoughts in diaries or journals.

3. Write a short story titled "The Holiday I Would Like to Forget." Make a graph of your classmates' holiday selections. Look at the holiday that the most stories were written about. In your opinion, why does this occasion appear so often in "the memories I like to forget" of young children?

4. Find the names and addresses of three stores that sell diaries.

5. Make an acrostic poem titled "Diary Secrets."

6. Compare the personalities of Beezus and Ramona with two other sisters in the myths, legends and stories that you have read.

7. Write a newspaper article on how fashionable keeping a diary is. Make it sound to the reader that everyone should be keeping a diary.

8. Make an illustrated catalog and price guide of diaries that a shop customer might look through before purchasing a diary.

9. Design a T-shirt that would encourage someone to keep a diary or make fun of people who keep diaries.

10. Design an original "keep out of my diary" page.

11. Research Morse and other secret codes (like the alphabet code that appeared in Ramona's diary). Design a code of your own or present one of the ones you researched to your classmates.

12. Design a page of your diary where every other sentence is missing. Exchange your ideas with a friend and complete each other's diary pages.

13. What invention would you design that would make everyday writing or diary writing easier? One of my students designed a vocal diary. You speak into the machine, and it writes in your diary for you.

14. Write a dialogue between Beezus and Ramona where Beezus accuses Ramona of writing in her diary.

GA1329

Teacher Suggestions

1. Make a classroom mural titled "Best Diary Doodles."

2. Contact your local police station and arrange for a class visit by a handwriting expert. Send him/her a list of questions that your children have about handwriting. Also include questions about writing analysis and its use in solving crimes. Lie detector questions always appear here.

3. Have your class design a fun park around the theme of writing, literature or children's diaries. You might want to start your class with designing a ride that would be fashioned after a nursery rhyme or children's story.

4. Research the nicknames of famous people in history with your class. Make a chart with the funniest, best and most unusual nicknames.

5. Discuss and show examples of caricatures to your students. Have them analyze what the artist is exaggerating, or have your class determine the most outstanding feature of the picture subjects that you will show them.

6. There are some tremendous outdoor geometry activities in the "Madison Project" books that usually are floating around most schools. Combine these with the outdoor game section of *The Ramona Quimby Diary*.

7. Divide the class in half. One half of the class collects phrases that have *happy* (happy birthday) in them, while the other half collects phrases that have *good* (good-bye) in them.

8. Have a Bring an Imaginary Pet to School Day. Each child draws and describes his imaginary pet to his classmates. Make an imaginary pet zoo on one of your bulletin boards.

9. Have your class design the ideal school bus stop—a place where all children definitely wouldn't mind waiting for the school bus.

10. Researching the hairstyles of the Presidents' wives goes well with "Beezus, a seventh grade girl with forty-year-old hair." Changing tastes in fashion can also be discussed.

11. "Biting a girl's eraser in half is a sure sign of love." What other signs of love can you discern with your students?

12. What type of company would be used to design a playground? Are there any stone quarries near your school? How about cement factories? Design a thinking web with your class showing all the industry connected with building a playground, school or any other appropriate project.

GA1329

Write Like a Master

Complete the three short story starters below with the theme that a diary is in some way involved with solving the problems presented. Your approach can be humorous or serious.

Story Starter I

It happened last week and the week before. Three weeks ago it happened twice. It can't be a coincidence. Everything that I wish for in my diary happens exactly one week later—almost to the exact hour that I wrote it! Should I tell someone? Is there some way to conduct a test that would verify what I think is happening? Should I write something good and bad to see if both will happen? Do I _____

_____

_____

_____

_____

Story Starter II

There has to be something in this house that will give us a clue to what happened. It looks like the house has been untouched for years. This can't be true, because we were just here last week for Joan's daughter's wedding. The grounds and the house were spotless. This doesn't even look like the same place. It is scary that Joan's picture looks like it has aged while hanging in the foyer. Maybe this old box and the book in it will give us some clues. It looks like a hundred-year-old diary. It says _____

_____

_____

_____

_____

Story Starter III

A poem diary! I never heard of anything like it. Is it a book of famous poems, or is it a book of personal thoughts that are in poem form? Wow! When you think of it, you reach the conclusion that a person would have to be a genius to put all of his/her thoughts into poetic form. I could probably do acrostics of the events in my life, but rhyme or prose everything? No way! This first entry is about a birthday party and it is really done well. The person writing it really had a good time. See if you can decide if the person was invited to the party or if the party was for the writer. Listen to the _____

_____

_____

_____

_____

33

GA1329

Henry and the Clubhouse

Newspaper Route

Bathtub Rides

Beezus and Ramona

Dog Problems

Clubhouse Pals

34

Lead-Ins to Literature

A new clubhouse, trouble with a paper route, pets, Beezus and Ramona, the Sheriff Bud Show and new neighbors all combine to make Henry Huggins' life exciting, humorous and sometimes challenging. From riding in a bathtub to dressing up for Halloween, you will be amazed how Henry turns each small event into a major happening. Maybe you will find things in your life that will match Henry's minor adventures. You'll also notice that Ramona and Beezus are interesting enough to have books written about them, also.

1. What kind of clubhouse did you have in mind when you read the title to this book?

2. What kind of club would you have formed to make use of your clubhouse?

3. Paper routes are one way children can make money. Can you think of any other ways children can earn money?

4. Pets are always troublesome in stories. What type of troubles would you write for the pets in this story if you were the author?

5. Would you be willing to deliver papers every day in the rain, snow, heat and cold?

6. How would you have the girls down the street (Ramona and Beezus) annoy Henry Huggins?

7. Do you think girls need praise more than boys?

8. What is the best way for parents to compliment and praise their children?

9. Knowing that Henry is a struggling paper boy, how would you have him deliver papers? Wagon? Bike? Car? Scooter?

10. What kind of dog fits best in a clubhouse story? Why?

GA1329

Vexing Vocabulary

journal	shadow	stretchers
subscriptions	upholstery	disguises
jeers	ridiculous	exasperated
arguing	geraniums	garage
enthusiasm	snarling	primary
assured	confident	businesslike
allowance	sheriff	Ramona
pestering	coaxed	impression

Your writing and vocabulary usage will be put to the ultimate test in this "literature mad-lib." Twenty-four vocabulary words and numerous blanks have been provided for you. You may not change the location of any of the words or blanks. The blanks indicate where you may put words of your own to complete the story. Pick a theme, title and then form a story around the words already given to you. Good luck! You will need it!

Complete these short sentences before trying the story.

1. _____ jeers _____ _____ _____ confident.

2. Geraniums _____ _____ coaxed _____ _____ _____.

3. _____ Sheriff _____ _____ _____ shadows.

4. _____ Ramona exasperates _____ _____ _____.

5. _____ _____ _____ garage _____ _____ businesslike _____.

Now you are ready to try your hand at the story.

_____
(title)

"_____ pestering _____," snarled Ramona. You _____ _____ _____ _____ _____ impression. _____ primary _____ _____ coaxed _____ _____ _____ ridiculous disguise _____ Sheriff _____. _____ assured _____ businesslike _____ _____ enthusiasm. _____ confident _____ _____ *Journal* subscriptions _____ _____ _____ _____ _____ garage. _____ _____ _____ allowance _____ _____ upholstery _____ stretchers. _____ jeers _____ _____ _____ shadows _____ _____ geraniums _____ _____ _____ exasperated _____.

Try writing some sentences with blanks and vocabulary words for one of your classmates. Have a sentence in mind just in case you stump him and he challenges you for an answer.

GA1329

Just the Facts

1. What were the names of Henry's dog and cat? _____
2. What paper did Henry deliver in his neighborhood? _____
3. Where was the bathtub being delivered? _____
4. Who had to deliver Henry's papers? _____
5. What was wrong with Mr. Bingham's garage? _____
6. What did Henry and his dog dress up as on Halloween? _____
7. What type of dog was Ranger? _____
8. What was Ramona always reciting? _____
9. What was Mrs. Morgan's gift to Henry? _____
10. How is a dog different from a flea? _____
11. What dangerous trick did Ramona play on Henry in the clubhouse? _____
12. Dad gave Henry five dollars. What was he going to use it for? _____
13. Who was Ramona's favorite person? _____

Write five questions and answers about the story to challenge your classmates.

1. _____
2. _____
3. _____
4. _____
5. _____

RANGER

GA1329

 # What Is Your Opinion?

1. Did you think Henry was right in banning girls from joining his club?

   _____

   _____

2. Do you think Mr. Grumbie should have allowed Henry to ride in the bathtub in the back of his trailer?

   _____

   _____

3. If you were Henry, wouldn't you have escorted Beezus home instead of allowing her to cross streets on her own?

   _____

   _____

4. Some people don't feel comfortable selling things, even if they are only newspaper subscriptions. Was there any way Henry could have gotten out of going door to door to ask people to buy his paper?

   _____

   _____

5. What do you think makes Halloween so enjoyable for children of all ages?

   _____

   _____

6. Was a stuffed owl the most unusual Halloween treat that you ever heard about? What else was as unusual?

   _____

   _____

7. How would you have handled someone like Mrs. Peabody who always said your name incorrectly?

   _____

   _____

8. Ramona always knew what time it was even though she couldn't tell time or read? How was this possible?

   _____

   _____

9. Who was more likable, Ramona or Henry? Why?

   _____

   _____

10. Was Henry's letter to Sheriff Bud, even though it worked in reverse, a creative idea? Why didn't it work?

    _____

    _____

11. Was there a better way Henry's dad could have rewarded Henry instead of giving him money?

    _____

    _____

GA1329

Ideas and Illustrations

Below you will find the partial outlines of Henry's clubhouse. One outline deals with how the clubhouse might look if it were in a tree. The other is a clubhouse in Henry's yard. Complete each picture and fill in the extra ideas that would go in such a scene.

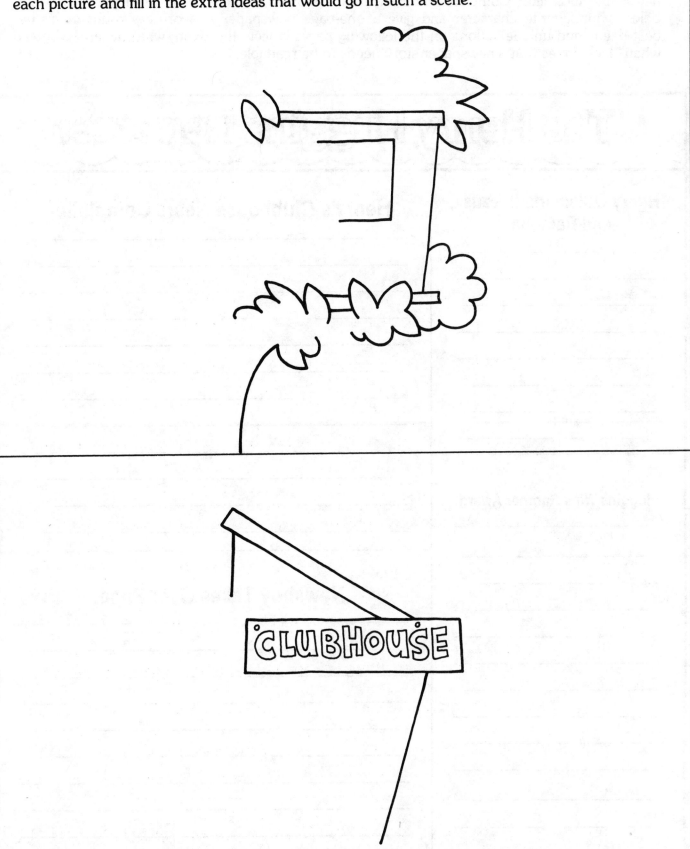

39

Short-Term Project

Would it be possible to make the front page of a newspaper completely about the antics of your favorite character from children's books? If you could, what would a Henry Huggins' newspaper look like? Complete and illustrate the stories on the front page of this newspaper. Select your favorite character and give a one-page newspaper's flavorful account of his/her best deeds and unique actions on the following page. Review the "who, what, where, why and when" techniques that a newspaper story needs to be readable.

The Henry Huggins Reporter

Henry Outsmarts Beezus and Ramona

_____
_____
_____
_____
_____
_____
_____

Huggins Wins Another Award

_____
_____
_____
_____
_____
_____
_____
_____
_____
_____

Henry's Clubhouse Nears Completion

_____
_____
_____
_____
_____
_____
_____
_____
_____
_____
_____
_____

Newsboy Takes Over Paper

_____
_____
_____
_____
_____
_____
_____
_____

GA1329

Short-Term Project
Student Sheet

Would it be possible to make the front page of a newspaper completely about the antics of your favorite character from children's books? If you could, what would a newspaper about your favorite character look like? Complete and illustrate stories about your character on the front page of this newspaper form. Focus on your character's best deeds and unique actions. Make your headlines and stories serious and humorous. Review the "who, what, where, why and when" techniques that a newspaper story needs to be readable.

Newspaper Subject _____

Newspaper Title _____

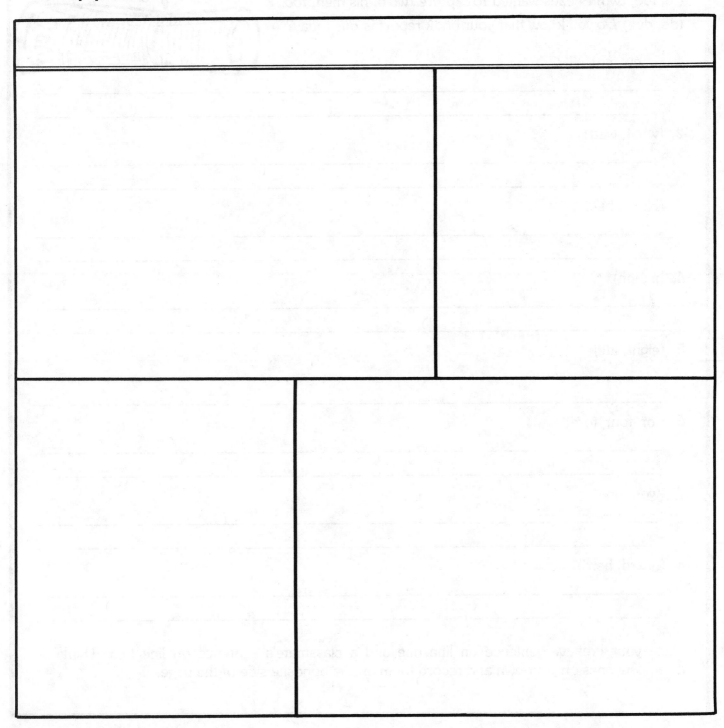

GA1329

Too Tough for You Two to Do
Drills for Skills

Henry had to be good in his *sales* attempts for the *Journal*. Henry's mom *sails* the papers all over the lawn. *Sales/Sails* are homonyms, and it is quite easy to write them each in a sentence. Your homonym ability will be challenged as you try to write each of these homonym pairs from *Henry and the Clubhouse* in one sensible sentence. Study the examples below before trying to write sentences on your own.

Examples:

(reel, real) The broken *reel* made it *real* hard to land the fish.

(to, too, two) Beezus wanted *to* capture *two* of his men, *too*.

(do, due) *Do* you know that your book report is *due* today?

1. (know, no)

_____

_____

2. (what, watt)

_____

_____

3. (Hugh, hue)

_____

_____

4. (in, inn)

_____

_____

5. (eight, ate)

_____

_____

6. (for, four, fore)

_____

_____

7. (won, one)

_____

_____

8. (heard, herd)

_____

_____

Place your creative sentence on line one and a classmate's sentence on line two. Think of three new ones on your own and record them on the opposite side of the page.

Research Suggestions

1. Research the clubs in your area. How many are there and what are their membership rules like?

2. Design a class newspaper and a campaign to advertise it. If you have a computer, *The Children's Writing Center* by The Learning Company is an easy and enjoyable way to design your class newspaper's stories and format.

3. Interview a dog trainer or handler to learn some dog training techniques that you can share with your class. Tell him/her about Ribsy and Ranger's fight and ask for suggestions on how to handle the situation.

4. What type of dirty water recycling is done in your town? How many car washes and industrial plants use this type of water? What is done in your area to conserve water? Have you noticed any water pollution in your area? What do you think are minor water problems that may turn into major ones?

5. Believe it or not there are many types of animals that you cannot kill and stuff. Most of them fall in the threatened or endangered species category, but some do not. See what animals are protected in such a way in your area.

6. Do a modes of transportation survey and find the number and percentage of students who come to school by foot, bicycle, car, bus, train, taxi, van, etc.

7. Henry yelled, "Open, sesame" which comes from the story "Ali Baba and the Forty Thieves." Can you think of any other statements that we use that would come from stories we have read? "Off with their heads," "I'll get that rabbit," etc. Make a list of the statements and their originators.

8. Present the three top commercials on TV and radio. Have your classmates vote on which one they think is the most creative. Research commercial jingles. Are there any that people are now singing or humming in Ramona's fashion?

9. Do a Saturday morning cartoon survey. Find out which cartoons are watched the most. Do this for three different age groups.

10. Henry wrote to Sheriff Bud and Mrs. Peabody wrote to the *Journal.* Design a writing campaign and find five places that children can send their writing. See if members of your class can send ideas and opinions to the editorial page of your local newspaper.

11. Design a speech that you will give at someone's house as you try to persuade the house owner to buy your local newspaper. Show the paper's best sections as you present.

o **Research**
o **Design**
o **Interview**
o **Present**

GA1329

Teacher Suggestions

1. Contact your local newspaper to find out what services they have available for school groups. In Philadelphia the newspapers have a special educational handbook of activities and an educational supplement that comes out once a week. Your class might want to write an educational page on a particular topic for your local newspaper.

2. Develop with your class the difference between a lead character and a minor character. Make a three-part chart using your children's favorite stories . . . . their lead characters . . . . their minor characters. Have your class compare minor characters and discuss their importance to each story. Give a pre-designed book award to the best one.

3. Make a chart of the types of animals you find in children's stories. Discuss what animals are most common and which ones would be considered unique by their appearances or actions.

4. Have a Halloween in May party with your class. Each child is responsible for creatively dressing up as one of the months of the year. How about a Dress Up Your Pet Day. Children dress up their pets and take pictures of them to be displayed on a classroom bulletin board. There is a film called *The Twelve Seasons* that you might want to show the class before planning your months-of-the-year party.

5. Research with your class the steps in starting a small business compared with those you'd need to follow to start a club.

6. The lock business is a fascinating one from your local locksmith and home builder to policeman. Invite one of them in to talk about new ideas in protecting your home, bike, clubhouse and other property. Many police divisions have property identification number programs and would gladly talk to school children or a parents' group about car and home protection.

7. Start a class advice column called "Dear Disgusted" or "Dear Amy" and write/exchange letters discussing community problems and their solutions.

8. How many brands of potato chips and nuts are there and how much does television influence what we eat are two good research topics.

9. Have your students make a headline notebook or collage capturing the three best headlines in the areas of community interest, politics, sports, religion, entertainment or fashion.

10. Have a fashion show for what the best-dressed paper boy or girl might wear while completing his/her paper deliveries.

GA1329

Write Like a Master

Complete the three short story starters below using the theme that some minor irritation or annoyance is growing out of proportion. It is *starting*, as they say in television creature stories, *to drive you crazy*. You need help but don't know where to turn because it probably will seem like nothing to anyone else who evaluated your situation.

Story Starter I
Thud! Now, it is on my roof! This makes thirteen days in a row, and he still doesn't have it right. If I find my newspaper in one more weird location other than my front steps, my paper boy may not see his next birthday. Just joking, of course . . . . But something has to be done. I don't want to get him fired. He is working his way through night school. Maybe I should

_____

_____

_____

_____

Story Starter II
Nasty little pests buzzing in my ear, ruining my sleep, outdoor reading and family picnic on the same weekend. The weather man said that the April rains caused this overabundance of flies. The local science columnist said that flies never fly more than 300 feet (91 m) from their nests. Judging from the number that are around my house, this must be central headquarters for "Flyville Junction." Maybe I should _____

_____

_____

_____

_____

Story Starter III
This club just doesn't have any zip. The clubhouse looks like an old washing machine and our club song sounds like something the Three Stooges would sing. Our flag is in tatters and our watchdog doesn't even growl when strangers approach. We need some new ideas. Maybe we should _____

_____

_____

_____

_____

45

Creative Story Writing
Dear Mr. Henshaw

Losing Bandit

Stolen Lunches

Letters to My Favorite Author

A Lovable Stray Dog

Long Trips Away from Home

Lead-Ins to Literature

Could keeping a diary, writing to a pen pal or communicating by letter with your favorite author change your life? Can people that you have never met in person have a greater effect on your life than those around you? What attributes would this faraway person have to keep your interest? Do you think humor could possibly be a force that brings faraway people together in this story?

1. Did the name Mr. Henshaw bring any mental images to mind before reading this story? For some reason I thought he was either a teacher or a magician. What did you think his occupation might have been before you read the story?

2. From the picture on the book's cover, it is easy to see that letter writing might play an important part in this story. What three ways would you incorporate letter writing into the theme of a story you were writing?

3. Have you read any other children's stories where written messages or letters played an important part in the story? Look at *Alice in Wonderland* and the countless messages and little notes that made her tale so much more enjoyable.

4. Can you list five reasons why someone would keep a diary? What are five good reasons for not keeping a diary?

5. If you could write to any author, who would you choose? Select a male and female. Why did you choose those particular authors?

6. Beverly Cleary, like Judy Blume, often develops the theme of a new kid in school or in the neighborhood. What are three advantages and disadvantages of being a "new kid"?

7. There are many occupations like truck driver and airplane pilot that would keep a parent away from home a large amount of time. What advice would you give a friend who was concerned about how often his/her parents are away from home? What advice would you give to the often absent parent to better meet the needs of his/her family?

8. In the story you will meet a dog named Bandit. Can you think of three reasons why a person would name his/her dog Bandit?

9. If you were an author, how would you use the idea of "missing lunch box food" in one of your stories?

10. What do you know about burglar alarm systems? Where would these systems be used?

47

GA1329

Vexing Vocabulary I

One of the goals of the vocabulary sections in this book is to make you aware of the important words in each story. A second goal is to teach you how to train yourself in recording and studying words you don't know or should know. You should begin keeping a word journal for each book that you read. Word journals by category look professional. The word journal below has been started for you. Add three words to each category from *Dear Mr. Henshaw* or from your own experience. Add four additional categories and five words from each to represent *Dear Mr. Henshaw* in your journal. Share your list with a classmate.

Trucks	School	Kitchen	Street
vehicle	chalk	microwave	intersection
route	teacher	counter	traffic
loading	recess	refrigerator	highway
axle	aisle	disposal	signal
tune-up	principal	blender	accident
load	computer	refrigerator	block
spare	compass	coils	bridge
_____	_____	_____	_____
_____	_____	_____	_____
_____	_____	_____	_____

My four *Dear Mr. Henshaw* categories and words are as follows:

1. _____   2. _____   3. _____   4. _____

Did you ever keep a journal of characters in your readings? People in the news? Sports figures? Explorers?

GA1329

Vexing Vocabulary II

beggar	Columbia River	refinery
howled	amuse	minus
argument	fancy	talented
refrigerated	gondolas	starve
Yellowstone Park	complain	burglar
nuisance	citizens	waitress
sagebrush	thief	lantern
hopefully	librarian	honorable

Choose eight of the vocabulary words above and record the sentence where they appear in the story. Underline the vocabulary word in the sentence and record its page number.

1. _____ Page _____
2. _____ Page _____
3. _____ Page _____
4. _____ Page _____
5. _____ Page _____
6. _____ Page _____
7. _____ Page _____
8. _____ Page _____

Choose eight new words. List two synonyms next to each word. One should come from your knowledge and the other from a thesaurus.

Word	**Knowledge**	**Thesaurus**
1. _____	_____	_____
2. _____	_____	_____
3. _____	_____	_____
4. _____	_____	_____
5. _____	_____	_____
6. _____	_____	_____
7. _____	_____	_____
8. _____	_____	_____

Can you use the remaining eight words in four sentences? Each sentence will have two words in it.

1. _____
2. _____
3. _____
4. _____

GA1329

Just the Facts

1. What grade was Leigh in when he first wrote Mr. Henshaw? _____

2. What is Mr. Henshaw's first name? _____

3. What was Leigh's grade on his book report about *Ways to Amuse a Dog*? _____

4. Leigh hates answers like *we'll see*. Who keeps on telling him this? _____

5. Leigh doesn't have a lot of friends in his new school. What does his mother call him because of this? _____

6. What do kids who have their teeth straightened have to wear? _____

7. Hermiston is near the Columbia River. In what state is Hermiston located? _____

8. What city did Leigh's dad visit in New Mexico? _____

9. The boys' selections for the young writers' yearbook seemed to revolve around monsters, lasers and outer space. What themes did the girls use for their selections? _____

10. What was the voltage on the battery that Leigh needed to protect his lunch box? _____

11. After Leigh's lunch box demonstration in the lunchroom, he thought this rating might no longer be descriptive of him. What was the rating? _____

12. Mr. Henshaw explains to Leigh in a letter that a character in a story should solve a problem or go through some sort of change. What was the name of Leigh's character that melted until he became a puddle? _____

13. What writing honor did the story "A Day on Dad's Rig" earn? _____

14. How did Mrs. Badger describe Boyd Henshaw to Leigh? _____

15. Who was Bonnie? _____

What Is Your Opinion?

1. What percentage of people in your class do you think have at one time or another written in a diary or journal? _____

2. Can you list some benefits of writing every day? Do you think all students would benefit from such a writing program? _____

3. Did you think Mr. Fridley's lunch box alarm idea was serious, or was he joking? _____

4. Why do you think Leigh's mom is against his hanging around any place? Couldn't he learn something at the gas station or stores near his home? _____

5. When Bandit jumped into Leigh's dad's cab in Nevada, nothing was done to find his real owner. Did you think this was proper? What options are open to someone who finds something that has to belong to someone else, be it animal, money, jewelry or some other prized possession? _____

6. Do you think it is fair to keep a dog cooped up in a house all day while the family is at work and at school? _____

7. In what cases would an animal be better company than a human? _____

8. What do you think the hardest part of being a trucker would be? Easiest part? Most enjoyable? _____

9. Do you think people that have "hearts bigger than a football stadium" are rare or commonplace? _____

10. Mr. Henshaw seems to have become Leigh's idol. Do you think writers are better idols than ball players or movie stars? _____

11. What suggestions could you offer that would make Leigh's lunch box alarm even better? _____

12. Do you think a lunch box alarm is an extreme measure? Could the lunch box problem have been solved in an easier manner? _____

13. What are the three biggest problems in your school that kids could help solve? _____

14. There were many funny, joyful and sad parts to Leigh's life in this story. Which one sticks out in your mind when you think of these three ideas? _____

15. How would you have felt with your father so far away from home so often? _____

GA1329

Ideas and Illustrations

The trucking business plays an important part in *Dear Mr. Henshaw*. Imagine that you, your mom, your dad and your brother and sister each own a truck in the family trucking business. Each carries a different type of product and is designed differently. After reviewing the designs of various trucks in your town or city, use the four truck outlines below to design trucks that four members of your family own. Try to personalize and make your truck logo or company insignia as creative as possible on each drawing. Make a scrapbook that contains ten national or local truck or van companies (Ryder, Roadway, Hertz, Acme, etc.) as a follow-up to this activity.

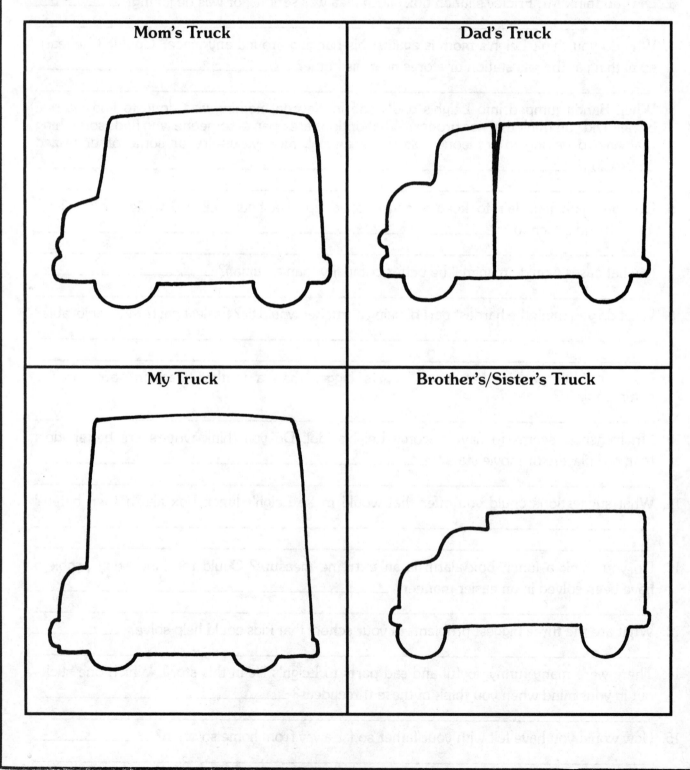

Mom's Truck

Dad's Truck

My Truck

Brother's/Sister's Truck

GA1329

Fictional Character Interview Directions and Examples
Short-Term Project
Student Directions

The following interview form has been designed to help you gather information to build a character sketch for future storytelling. Try to collect information that is not commonplace. Put your ideas down in short phrases that will give your writing a head start on someone that just records one-word answers in his interview. Pick two fictional characters from the list below. Conduct imaginary interviews with them. Add three questions to each category in the interview. Make sure that your questions will give additional information that you feel is necessary for creating an interesting character. Make up unique answers for the questions that have no real basis of information. Examples: Cinderalla was enrolled in what grade? She was about to begin night school in what subject? Where were she and the Prince planning to go on their honeymoon? What was her favorite song of those played at the ball? Did she like cleaning with a broom or cloth? Did she have other colors of dresses to go with her glass slipper? What kind of food was served at the ball? Was it a sit-down dinner or buffet? Did she live in a row house or an apartment? Who were her nonanimal friends? Of her two sisters, did she have a better relationship with the older or younger one? Did she have any time to play cards or board games when she wasn't working? Where did she shop?

The form on the following page has a format that will allow you to jot down questions based on actual information, as well as, questions that have no basis of information. If you can't find two of your favorite characters listed below, add new one's to the list.

1. Robin Hood
2. King Arthur
3. Sherlock Holmes
4. Queen of Hearts
5. Ramona Quimby
6. Henry Huggins
7. Paul Bunyan
8. Superman
9. Dick Tracy
10. Rapunzel
11. Peter Pan
12. Mother Goose
13. Sheila the Great
14. Hercules
15. Cupid
16. Jason/Golden Fleece
17. Reluctant Dragon
18. Icarus
19. Little Red Riding Hood
20. Pinocchio
21. Cinderella
22. Batman
23. Care Bears
24. Little Boy Blue
25. Tom Thumb
26. The Tin Soldier
27. Wicked Witch/West
28. Supergirl/Lois Lane

was enrolled in what grade? ☐ favorite song of those pla...

Did she like cleaning with a broom or cloth?

GA1329

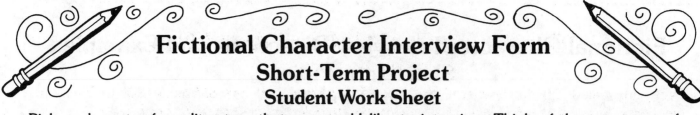

Fictional Character Interview Form
Short-Term Project
Student Work Sheet

Pick a character from literature that you would like to interview. Think of the two types of questions that you can ask your character. The first type is one where an answer can be found from the character's imaginary story. The second type is a question where the story really doesn't give you any information or basis to answer the question. You, therefore, will have to stretch your mind to write a question and to predict the character's answer. Review the questions asked of Cinderella on the previous page. Think of an answer that you might have written for each one. Listen to some of the ideas your classmates have before beginning the interview. Try writing humorous, as well as, serious questions and answers.

Your name _____

Character being interviewed _____

Place interview was conducted _____

Time of interview _____

Appearance of subject _____

Two factual/two nonfactual questions/answers for each area

Childhood

_____

_____

_____

Story Events

_____

_____

_____

Personal Questions—Likes/Dislikes

_____

_____

_____

Future Goals and Activities

_____

_____

_____

Choose an area of your own. _____

_____

_____

_____

GA1329

This Activity Is Old Hat or Brand-New
Drills for Skills

Each clue below can be answered by a word or phrase that has *old* or *new* in it. Find out what fraction is formed by placing the vowels over total letters in each word or phrase.

Clue	Answer	Vowels/Total Letters
1. Not hot		
2. Past tense of *know*		
3. Salamander		
4. Our flag		
5. Gravity + (apple)		
6. To yell at		
7. Brave		
8. Nixon's V.P.		
9. Bend paper		
10. Recyclable		
11. Card game		
12. Precious metal		
13. Just purchased		
14. Geyser		
15. Form		

Can you write five clues of your own that will generate a "new or old word"? Challenge your classmates with your work. Can you suggest a similar theme using other word pairs?

Research Suggestions

1. What are four of the major trucking firms in your area?

2. Is there a Big Brother or Sister group in your area? What type of activities do they conduct, and what children would benefit from them?

3. Bandit seemed to be a stray dog. What kind of agencies in your area handle strays? Do you have a Society for the Prevention of Cruelty to Animals in your town? Find out about the society's membership and activities.

4. Many big cities have an Adopt This Animal column in the paper each day. Design such a column using pictures of your pets or cutouts from magazines. Put your byline on the column and make it as professional looking as possible.

5. Research the missing person's procedure at your local police station. Design a missing person's column for a newspaper. Missing person notices appear on milk cartons. Research the procedure for getting a missing community member listed in such a way. How does this listing differ from the ten most wanted list that you can find at your post office?

6. How would one go about getting a patent on a lunch box alarm? Research the difference between a patent and a copyright. How do these relate to the FBI warning you see on the films that you rent from the local video store?

7. Research the experience and schooling that are needed to drive a trailer or big truck. Find out the difference in salary in owning your own truck or working for a trucking company.

8. Pick three minor crimes (stealing someone's lunch) and research the different penalties for them for a ten, sixteen or twenty-year-old.

9. Draw a section map of the United States, including your state and those around it. Draw some of the major highways and compare the speed limits from each state.

10. Research the ten most-read writers in your school and at the local bookstore. Do this for adults and children. If there is a publishing company nearby, research how the cost of a book is determined and the procedure for getting a manuscript read and a book published.

Teacher Suggestions

1. It is a long truck haul. Write the dialogue that would be spoken between a father and son or mother and daughter during one short period of the trip.

2. Write a letter to a trucking company asking for:
   a. company background
   b. types of jobs
   c. job qualifications
   d. company logos and patches
   e. company hats and stickers
   f. suggested speakers and topics
   g. trip availability at local facility
   h. how computers are used in their business
   i. employment—number of women employed, etc.

3. Lunch pails are often taken for granted, even though millions of people use them every day.
   a. Find the three principal makers of lunch pails.
   b. Research the divisions that a lunch pail company has. The art and design division would be an important one in the children's market.
   c. What materials are used? Is there any advantage of using metals instead of plastics? Are the companies using renewable and recyclable materials?

4. Research stories where the children visit or interact with parents at the parents' jobs.

5. Make a list of authors that the class would like to write to. Write to one a week in care of their book company.

6. Have an Author Covered Dish Luncheon. Each child brings in a covered dish and explains why that dish is related to a certain author or story by that particular author. Most teachers do this with the child's favorite country. It works just as well with an author or favorite character from literature. Alice and the Queen of Hearts could bring tarts or cookies for dessert. Tom Thumb could bring plum pudding. Jack from beanstalk fame could bring roast beef or hot dogs and beans. Little Miss Muffit could bring cottage cheese (curd) and fruit. The man in the moon could bring cheese. The list can go on and on. Developing the list is just as enjoyable as the party and presentations.

7. Research what information bulletin boards are available in your area. Even though you may not have a computer in your room or school, this information can be printed for you and shared with your class.

8. Have a bookstore owner come to your classroom to present the latest selections and age-old classics of children's books.

GA1329

Write Like a Master

Complete the three short story starters below using the theme that a personal letter has generated some change in the lead character's life, present situation or personality. Try to be different in your approach. Discuss ideas with two classmates and make thoughts completely different from theirs.

Story Starter I

Irregular heartbeats are not at all commonplace in my family. Yet as I walked to the mailbox my heart seemed to be signaling a "life-threatening" alert. My feet felt heavy as the distance to the mailbox lessened. The letter was sitting address down, certainly a sign of bad luck. My hands trembled as I opened the letter. My worst fears were soon to be realized. _____

_____

_____

_____

_____

Story Starter II

The laugh probably should have been a cry. I couldn't believe the letter in my hand. Why would someone want to do that to me? Why in a letter of all things? The least they could have done is sign it. At least, then, my anger could be channeled toward someone rather than a "concerned friend." Why would someone want to bring up something that happened years ago? Something that few people will understand! _____

_____

_____

_____

_____

Story Starter III

The letter made me happier than my wildest dreams. It didn't even bother me that it wasn't very well written. The miles the letter travelled showed on the envelope. The postmark hinted of great adventures. Now it was my turn for adventure! _____

_____

_____

_____

_____

GA1329

Lead-Ins to Literature

Everyone thinks that his dog is the best dog in the whole world. It wasn't unusual, then, for Henry Huggins to feel the same way about his dog Ribsy. Losing the best dog in the world is, of course, going to upset Henry. If you have ever lost something that you loved, you will know how Henry feels as he searches for his dog. If you've ever been lost, you will understand what Ribsy is going through. Good authors write stories that bring out the reader's emotions, but what if Ribsy is lost forever? How will Henry deal with the situation and will Ribsy enjoy his new home?

1. What three adventures would you put a lost dog through in a story like this?

   _____

2. What are three things you would advise Henry to do in helping him in his search to find his lost dog?

   _____

3. Is this the type of story where you have a dogcatcher chasing Ribsy at the same time Henry is looking for him to make the story a little more dramatic? Explain why you would or wouldn't do this if you were the author?

   _____

4. How do you think Henry lost his dog? Tell how you would have described the scene where Ribsy is lost.

   _____

5. Will the author give Ribsy a girlfriend or animal companion to make the story more interesting or to make you believe Ribsy is never coming home?

   _____

6. How might the reader feel if the story doesn't have a happy ending where Henry and Ribsy are united?

   _____

7. What stories have you read that didn't have happy endings? Have you recently read a story where you tried to predict the ending and it was completely the opposite of how you thought it would end?

   _____

8. Make a list of five completely different endings that a good author could use to end this story.

   _____

9. Would you accept the offer of another needy dog if your dog were lost for more than two weeks? If you were the author, how long would you keep the dog missing and would you return it to Henry at the end of the story? Explain. (One of my students said that the new family might need a dog, say for a very sick child, more than Henry and in that case they would keep the dog missing.)

   _____

10. Are dog collars mandatory in your town or city? What information is normally found on a collar? Where do you have one made with the relevant information included?

    _____

11. Find out what is on an army dog tag.

    _____

Vexing Vocabulary I

Twenty-four vocabulary words are written to the left of the lines below. Follow your teacher's directions as he/she sends you on a scavenger hunt to find the exact sentence and page number where each word appears. Your teacher will pay the winning team one million dollars. Good luck!

menacingly   1. _____ Page ___

gratitude   2. _____ Page ___

infuriated   3. _____ Page ___

whimpered   4. _____ Page ___

pedigree   5. _____ Page ___

biscuit   6. _____ Page ___

scornful   7. _____ Page ___

obligingly   8. _____ Page ___

stadium   9. _____ Page ___

dawdling   10. _____ Page ___

bologna   11. _____ Page ___

macaroni   12. _____ Page ___

humane   13. _____ Page ___

upholstery   14. _____ Page ___

persistent   15. _____ Page ___

Pomeranian   16. _____ Page ___

automatic   17. _____ Page ___

cafeteria   18. _____ Page ___

photographer 19. _____ Page ___

bewildered   20. _____ Page ___

terrified   21. _____ Page ___

overheard   22. _____ Page ___

relented   23. _____ Page ___

eager   24. _____ Page ___

Scavenger Hunt

Vexing Vocabulary II

Each clue below will help you discover a word that has *rib* in it in exact order. When you find the correct word, square the number of letters in it and multiply it times the problem number to determine your word's value.

Clue	Answer	Value
1. A baby's resting place	_____	_____
2. Hair decoration	_____	_____
3. South American sea	_____	_____
4. North American deer	_____	_____
5. Illegal money offer	_____	_____
6. Card/Moving peg game	_____	_____
7. Indian family group	_____	_____
8. Bounce a basketball	_____	_____
9. Terrible/Gruesome	_____	_____
10. Small stream branch	_____	_____
11. Done to show respect	_____	_____
12. Often used newspaper name	_____	_____

Take the word *arm* and see how many clues you can write for words that have *arm* in them. Exchange your list of ten with a classmate. Tell him/her you want to do a little "arm" wrestling.

Clue	Answer	Value
1. _____	_____	_____
2. _____	_____	_____
3. _____	_____	_____
4. _____	_____	_____
5. _____	_____	_____
6. _____	_____	_____
7. _____	_____	_____
8. _____	_____	_____
9. _____	_____	_____
10. _____	_____	_____

GA1329

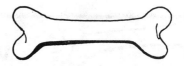

Just the Facts

Unscramble the key words in each sentence below and you will have "just the facts" from Beverly Cleary's *Ribsy*. Write the key word on the blank following each sentence.

1. When you have troubles with SAFEL, you have plenty of troubles. _____

2. Ribsy SKEHSA with his left paw. _____

3. Did you ever amuse yourself with SNITEN? _____

4. The parking lot was painted with ANDILOGA white lines. _____

5. STEVLIO certainly smell strong when they are all over someone. _____

6. The Klickitat Street mailman often said "LUNCOM FLET" when he had a big crowd following him. _____

7. Ribsy was not WAGGINN through the rope nor digging under the fence. _____

8. Joe was not in the refrigerator; he was feeding a stray dog in the INCHEKT. _____

9. Darlene could practice her AONIP more often. _____

10. Ribsy discovered that the IFRE PEASEC was frightening and uncomfortable. _____

11. Henry found Ribsy at a DOBY DAN DEERFN business. _____

12. One of the reasons Ribsy was lost for over a month was because he was LORLAC EFER.

_____

13. There definitely wasn't any quiet in the room, especially since there was a squirrel SOLOE.

_____

14. I can never remember the GELDEP FO CANGELELIA. _____

15. When people say, "hit the bricks," they probably really mean "hit the STALHAP." _____

Try taking five facts from *Ribsy* and putting them into sentences with a scrambled word in the spaces below. Trade your five with a neighbor to see who gets the most correct.

1. _____

2. _____

3. _____

4. _____

5. _____

What Is Your Opinion?

1. The first chapter in the book talks about fleas. Is there another way the author could have emphasized that Ribsy wasn't a purebred? By the way, how many times did you scratch while reading the first chapter? _____

2. What are some everyday safeguards that you can follow to protect your dog from wandering off or from dognappers? _____

3. Would you have left your dog in the car unattended, with the doors unlocked the way Henry did? Explain. Was his mistake one that anyone could have made? _____

4. What is the best part about being lost? The worst? _____

5. Are bubble baths overrated or as special as we often make them to be? Do you think our opinion of them started when we were very young? _____

6. Most authors cause trouble with the animals their characters bring to school. Are there any good sides to bringing animals into school? Are the situations these animals create always humorous in the stories you read? _____

7. Playing football is a neat trick for an animal. What is the most outstanding trick performed by an animal that you have seen on television, at the circus, in the zoo, at home or in your neighborhood? See if you can remember one in each category. Then pick your best choice of the five. _____

8. Of Ribsy's mini adventures, which one did you like the best? _____

9. Would you have cleared the classroom and called for a professional instead of going after a possible rabid carrying squirrel on your own? _____

10. How close are the actions of lost pets and lost children? _____

11. Was Henry's mother right to continue driving when she knew that the dog was still following them? _____

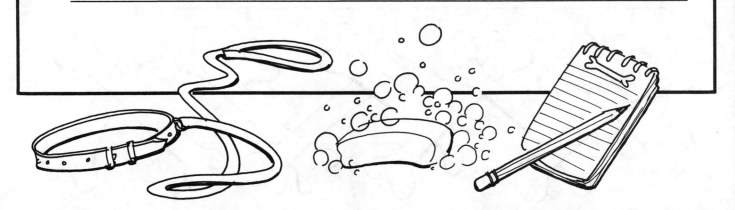

GA1329

From Head to Toe
Ideas and Illustrations

Four sections are provided for your "head to toe" creations. Cut out the heads of four different dogs from magazines, old books or newspapers. Mount them to the left of each box provided below. Cut out the bodies of four different animals and combine them with the dog heads. We originally put the dog heads on people's bodies. The results were so weird that I hesitate to suggest the idea in a book that my mother might read. Make up names for your new creatures and highlight some of their attributes. Do this a second time, but this time draw the rest of the body. Do not make it an animal. Try changing it into a piece of furniture, car, building or any strange but true design you can think to create.

Place your creature description below each of your illustrations.

65

GA1329

Short-Term Project

Cats, dogs and other animals are often used to describe people, situations and assorted events. Design an animal file below using eight creatures who are often used in descriptive phrases. Four files have been started for you. Illustrate your best sayings and make a mini display.

Cats
1. That car missed me by a cat's whisker!
2. I think I'll take a little catnap.
3. The baby is as playful as a kitten.

4. _____

Dogs
1. Doggone! That is a beautiful painting.
2. He is treated worse than a dog.
3. Bill is a real hot dog.

4. _____

Pigs
1. He is happier than a pig in slop.
2. Don't be a pig. Share your dessert.
3. Let's pig out on French fries at the drive-in stand.

4. _____

Birds
1. They are real birdbrains.
2. Betty has the eye of an eagle.
3. I don't give a hoot about homework.

4. _____

Your choice _____
1. _____
2. _____
3. _____
4. _____

Your choice _____
1. _____
2. _____
3. _____
4. _____

Your choice _____
1. _____
2. _____
3. _____
4. _____

Your choice _____
1. _____
2. _____
3. _____
4. _____

GA1329

Inside Outs
Drills for Skills
Student Page (Hard)

Inside Outs will stretch your vocabulary and critical thinking ability. Each square below has a nine-letter word hidden in it. The starting letter can be found in the middle square. The following letters are in exact order around the outside of the square. They may be read clockwise or counterclockwise after you go from the middle letter to the next letter in the hidden word. Place a dot next to the second letter in each word you have found and draw an arrow indicating what direction to walk with your eyes to determine the total word. Place your answers in the spaces provided below. Use the blank master on page 69 to create inside outs of your own to exchange with your classmates.

Example:

S	E	R
E	P	D
N	T	E

1.

R	T	A
E	E	I
T	N	N

2.

I	T	C
V	E	E
E	F	F

3.

M	U	L
I	S	A
D	E	T

4.

P	R	I
L	A	S
A	N	E

5.

L	U	F
L	C	E
Y	A	R

6.

P	A	R
H	G	G
Y	E	O

7.

L	O	M
I	K	E
R	E	T

8.

R	E	C
R	I	T
O	C	N

9.

N	O	I
D	E	T
U	C	A

10.

N	E	T
F	I	A
U	R	I

11.

E	S	S
D	E	C
A	P	A

Answers:

Example: presented

1. _____
2. _____
3. _____
4. _____
5. _____

6. _____
7. _____
8. _____
9. _____
10. _____
11. _____

GA1329

Inside Outs
Drills for Skills
Student Page (Easy)

1.

H	T	E
G	D	D
I	L	E

2.

T	I	S
E	O	O
S	P	P

3.

T	F	D
E	A	R
R	W	A

4.

A	R	E
M	H	G
B	U	R

5.

T	R	O
A	I	P
N	T	M

6.

R	E	D
E	W	H
P	S	I

7.

G	N	I
I	T	E
P	T	O

8.

O	I	T
N	S	A
I	T	U

9.

R	T	S
U	S	E
G	G	L

10.

E	L	L
W	S	T
R	I	A

11.

P	T	N
A	A	E
R	T	M

12.

E	R	T
N	S	S
U	O	U

13.

E	L	E
P	T	E
H	O	N

14.

T	E	O
A	F	R
N	U	T

15.

R	R	E
U	I	T
P	T	N

16.

A	T	T
I	S	R
L	H	I

Answers:

1. _____
2. _____
3. _____
4. _____
5. _____
6. _____
7. _____
8. _____

9. _____
10. _____
11. _____
12. _____
13. _____
14. _____
15. _____
16. _____

GA1329

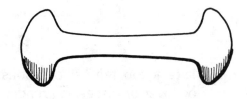

Inside Outs
Drills for Skills
Blank Master

Inside Outs will stretch your vocabulary and critical thinking ability. Each square below has a nine-letter word hidden in it. The starting letter can be found in the middle square. The following letters are in exact order around the outside of the square. They may be read clockwise or counterclockwise after you go from the middle letter to the next letter in the hidden word. Place a dot next to the second letter in each word you have found and draw an arrow indicating what direction to walk with your eyes to determine the total word.

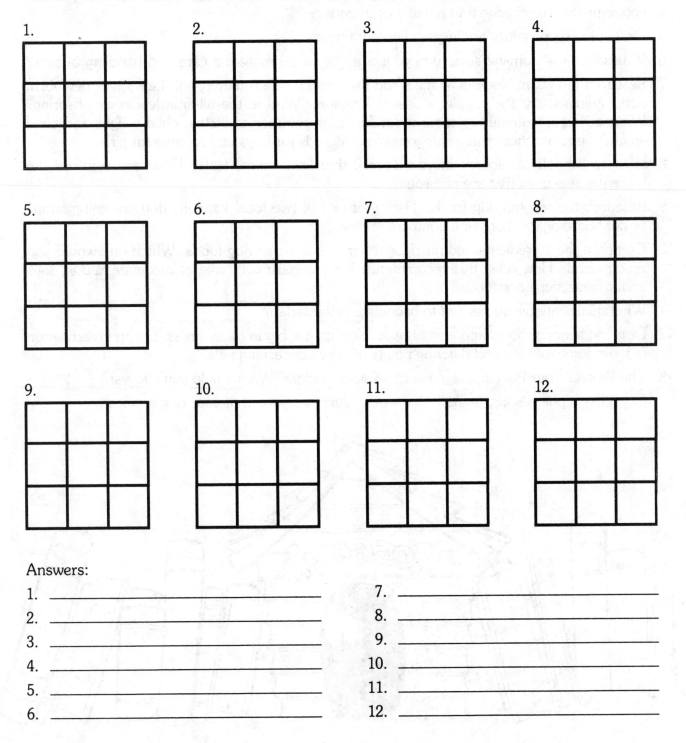

Answers:

1. _____   7. _____
2. _____   8. _____
3. _____   9. _____
4. _____   10. _____
5. _____   11. _____
6. _____   12. _____

Research Suggestions

1. Make a top ten list of books with enjoyable animals that you would recommend to any dog lover or discerning reader.

2. Research the ten most frequently picked names for dogs after canvassing the names of the dogs in your classroom and school.

3. What four new inventions could you design that would be used by any dog or dog owner? Create a pet invention for the home, car, school or yard. It does not have to be for just a dog.

4. What do you think is the most creative pet invention on the market today? How would you improve it or change it to make it even better?

5. Find out what penalties are imposed on pet thieves.

6. What does the humane society in your area do to promote the care and handling of pets?

7. Research ten warm-blooded animals and the general size (quantity) of their litters/newborn. After animals, try the reptile or insect kingdom. Who is the all-time leader in offspring? What are your community records for births in number of births, child weight and child length? Separate these three categories into records for boys and records for girls.

8. Is there a book of records in your library that lists animal feats? What are some of the more unusual ones that are recorded?

9. Research the top ten dog foods. Then visit or call two local kennels, dog grooming shops or pet boarding locations and compare choices.

10. Compare the ingredients and nutritional benefits of three dog foods. Which one would you recommend? How does this recommendation compare with what *Consumer Report* says about these same dog foods?

11. What qualifications are needed to become a veterinarian?

12. Dog obedience schools and animal psychologists are big in many areas. Do an investigation of their points of view and differing points of view concerning pets.

13. The Protect Your Pet campaign needs some new ideas. What would you suggest?

14. Compose a poem/song/limerick that would alert everyone that your dog was lost.

GA1329

Teacher Suggestions

1. The crisis of a lost pet is a serious one. Discuss with your class what other crises authors put animals and their owners through to increase the emotional response of the reader.

2. Famous people and their dogs make for interesting research and reading. Start your class with the Presidents and their pets before moving on to other areas.

3. Have your students compete in The Most Interesting Animal in Literature (Minotaur to Lassie) Contest. They must make their selections, present why their creatures should win the award and illustrate or diorama-ize their choices. The class will vote on the most interesting presentation at the conclusion of all the presentations. These make great classroom or hall displays.

4. Using the overhead projector and transparency paper, have your class enlarge their favorite pet, color it and make a size comparison chart comparing the enlarged animal to the actual size of the animal depicted.

5. The number of breeds and the history of dogs is an interesting topic. The Tell Me Why Science Series at your video store does an outstanding job introducing both topics. The Tell Me Why books can be found at most bookstores.

6. Have your class research animal speeds and compare speeds to various dogs and wolves. Quiz them on what family they think is faster, dog or cat. Young children guess dogs. Most older children know that the Cheetah is the fastest ground animal. Graph the size, weight and speed of classroom favorites. Mecc Graph is an excellent computer science program that allows the youngest of children to make major league charts.

7. Make a classroom mural titled "Dogs Have Feelings, Too." Solicit pictures of classroom pets in their most endearing poses. The children aways love the teacher bulletin board of matching teachers to their pictures when they were young. Have your fellow teachers bring in pictures of their pets. Number the pictures and place them on a bulletin board or in a trophy case. Give out the list of teacher names who handed in pictures. The child that matches the most pets to their owners is the winner.

8. Have your class design a Disneyland type ride with a dog as its theme.

9. Have a dog barking contest. It is hilarious!

10. Have your class research the clothing for pets industry.

11. What is the pet trade and is it endangering our animals worldwide? This makes a good class research project.

GA1329

Write Like a Master

The four short story starter themes below center around a very intelligent dog with uncanny abilities. When it comes to dealing with other animals and humans, your lead animal/character has no equal. Test your writing flexibility by trying to make at least one story serious and another one humorous. Make your dog points convincing.

Story Starter I
I hate cats. They always get more attention than the dogs in this household. Must be the way they purr. They certainly aren't very intelligent compared to my dogs. Why just the other day Barney, sweet cat that he is, got his tail caught in _____

_____

_____

_____

_____

Story Starter II
This invention will make humans forget about Snoopy, Lassie and Rin Tin Tin. It will revolutionize the ice-cream business and have every millionaire knocking on my doghouse door. That is, if I had a doghouse and it had a door. Come to think of it, maybe I should just invent a doghouse with a usable door. Enough of this side chatter. Let's talk ice cream. This invention will _____

_____

_____

_____

_____

Story Starter III
I really miss Chipper, probably more than my master Billy misses him. Billy cried for two days when they put Chipper to sleep, but only I knew how much pain Chipper was in. He told me about the pain, growing old and being unable to climb the stairs to sleep next to Billy in the bedroom. He said he missed sleeping next to Billy the most. I learned a lot from Chipper about _____

_____

_____

_____

_____

Story Starter IV
Let me give you a dog's point of view on why we are the most intelligent, dependable and lovable of creatures. It all starts with our ability to _____

_____

_____

_____

_____

72

GA1329

Fifteen

73

Lead-Ins to Literature

Did you ever wish that you wanted to meet someone new and presto, that very same day someone new walked into your life? If you weren't so happy, it would be frightening that your wish came true that quickly. This can cause problems. You know this person is fantastic, but how can you convince your parents the person isn't "the monster from beyond"? Parents don't buy things like "I have a good feeling," especially when you spent only two minutes with someone who sells horse meat door to door. What is even worse is the question "should you be yourself or the person you think they'll like?" That is if you knew who you really were. Sound confusing? Maybe it all gets straightened out in *Fifteen*.

1. If you were fifteen and wanted to meet new people, can you name five places other than the local hangout that would be good first-time meeting places (skating rink, bowling alley, bookstore, etc.) for new people?

   _____

2. Make a list of five things you'd like to do on a first date. Put the list away for a day. See if you can add five more choices to the list on the next day.

   _____

3. Who do you think is more nervous on a first date, the girl or the guy? Please explain.

   _____

4. Do you think parents should be cautious about who their children date, or do you think they should have enough confidence in their sons' and daughters' choices to go along with anything, sight unseen?

   _____

5. If you were a parent, would you meet all your child's dates before they went out? Please explain your feelings on this subject.

   _____

6. Are parents more protective of daughters or sons? Do you think they should be just as protective of both?

   _____

7. Do you have any friends who seem to be telepathic and know your thoughts before you do? How about a friend who can always read between the lines in your sentences? Did someone ever ask you what's wrong when you thought you were giving the appearance that nothing is wrong?

   _____

8. Should special thoughts be kept to yourself or shared with a friend? Please explain.

   _____

9. Can you name five benefits of baby-sitting?

   _____

10. Should there be other alternatives to horse meat for an ingredient in dog food?

   _____

11. How would you organize a toll free hot line for teenage dating questions? Could this be done on a local level?

   _____

GA1329

Vexing Vocabulary I

appendix
embarrassed
chrysanthemum
ominous
lurid
unoccupied
Shakespeare
mortuary

rumble seat
qualms
intrigued
gaiety
aromatic
harried
corduroy
appetite

astonishment
Capezio slippers
papier-mâché
bouquet
disapproval
Macbeth
martyrdom
Technicolor

Copy the twenty-four words in the blanks below. Tell what fraction and percent each word contains in vowels and letters made with only straight lines.

Vocabulary Word	% of Vowels	% of Straight Letters
1.		
2.		
3.		
4.		
5.		
6.		
7.		
8.		
9.		
10.		
11.		
12.		
13.		
14.		
15.		
16.		
17.		
18.		
19.		
20.		
21.		
22.		
23.		
24.		

Try writing five sentences. Each sentence must contain ten words. See what is the maximum number of vocabulary words that you can use in each ten-word sentence.

1. _____
2. _____
3. _____
4. _____
5. _____

GA1329

Initial Vocabulary
Vexing Vocabulary II

I am going to ask you a list of questions. Before I do that, you are to select three letters. The answer to each question must begin with the three letters you picked. Some teachers make you do the activity with your own initials. In this case, however, you can choose the three letters you feel will give you the greatest range for good answers.

Your name _____

Three letters or initials you picked _____

Example: Letters picked: STM

1. What is your name? Sandra Theresa Monahan

2. What is your hair like? short, tangly, messy

3. Who are your friends? Samantha, Tanya and Melanie

4. Name three things you like to do? _____

5. Where do you live? _____

6. What do you like to eat? _____

7. Do you have any travel plans? _____

8. What would be your choice of clothes? _____

9. What movies have you seen? _____

10. Name some books you have read. _____

11. What personal characteristics do you exhibit? _____

12. Name three islands you'd like to visit. _____

13. How would you describe your school successes? _____

14. In what period of history would you have liked to live? _____

15. Who is your favorite fictional character? _____

Pick six letters. You may not change their order. Write a sentence to answer each of the questions. Use the back of the page for your work. Letters picked: _____

1. Describe your best friend, a pet, a favorite spot.

2. What occupation are you pointing toward?

3. What do you like best about vacations?

4. Who would you like to change into?

5. What would you do on a first date?

GA1329

Just the Facts

1. Where was the worst baby-sitting job in Woodmont? _____

2. Counting convertibles and stepping on cracks were no ways to meet _____.

3. Who was Cuthbert? _____

4. What kind of ink was Sandra using to threaten Jane? _____

5. How do you say *go to sleep* in pig Latin? _____

6. What was Jane's usual order at Mr. Nibley's, and what did she order on her first date instead?

   _____

7. Mrs. Purdy didn't want Jane to run around with what type of crowd? _____

8. What toast did they all drink tea to at the Chinese restaurant in the city? _____

9. What was the first present that Stan bought Jane? _____

10. Jane was two inches taller than _____.

11. Who said, "Hence! Home, you idle creatures"? _____

12. What part of Stan's car did the girls want to ride in? _____

13. What is the lowest form of humor? _____

14. What hurt Stan and Julie's feelings? _____

15. _____ could probably be called masculine flowers.

Write a Just the Facts question about each of the following:

A. Stan Crandell _____

B. Mrs. Purdy _____

C. Mr. Purdy _____

D. The dance _____

E. Stan's dance date _____

F. Stan's car _____

G. 17 Poppy Lane _____

H. Shakespeare _____

Exchange your questions with a friendly competitor.

GA1329

What Is Your Opinion?

1. At what age should girls begin dating? Boys? Why?

   _____

2. Should there be a limit on the age of a person that a fifteen-year-old girl dates? Boy? Please explain.

   _____

3. Sandra Norton was a child that could use some help growing up. What would you have suggested for the "little monster"?

   _____

4. Do you believe in love at first sight? For yourself? Your friends?

   _____

5. Kids are forced to wear stupid costumes at many of the places they work. If they don't wear the costumes, they will lose jobs they really need. Would you suggest a formal protest, or would you just go along with the dress regulations? What other alternatives can you offer?

   _____

6. What is the best "I want to make up" present?

   _____

7. Who is the most memorable of the secondary characters in this story? Please explain why.

   _____

8. Would you give flowers to a boy? What not-overwhelming first present would you give to someone? List your five best choices.

   _____

9. Should Jane have talked to Stan long before the dance, or should she have gone to the dance alone?

   _____

10. Shouldn't all dances be singles only, no couples, so everyone can go and thousands of feelings and people won't be destroyed by thoughts of rejection?

    _____

11. Why shouldn't a girl have the same right to call a boy for a date as a boy calling a girl?

    _____

12. Would you date a person because of his/her car, clothes, friends or family, or would you base your dates on the type of person that date is with you?

    _____

13. If you get your own telephone, should you have to pay for the calls?

    _____

What five What Is Your Opinion questions would you like to pose to your classmates?

1. _____
2. _____
3. _____
4. _____
5. _____

78

GA1329

Ideas and Illustrations I

Charm bracelets are fun to collect. The business of designing necklaces/bracelets is a challenging one. You have to keep coming up with new designs that would attract necklace/bracelet owners. In the boxes below, design a charm or necklace piece to represent each of the occasions listed. Pick four months and design a birthday bracelet or necklace piece (like a birthstone) for yourself and three friends. Pick three occasions for which you have creative design ideas and include those, also.

Child's Name	Graduation	Wedding
Award	**Ballet**	**Religious**
Sports	**Academic**	**Club**
Theater	**TV**	**Birthday**

Use the reverse side of this paper for your ideas, or put them on 11″ x 14″ (27.94 x 35.56 cm) paper.

GA1329

Ideas and Illustrations II

Take a trip to the local Oriental rug store before completing the activity below. Research the various art tapestries/rugs that you can find in art books or at the local museum (the Philadelphia Museum of Art has twelve 20' x 20' [6.08 x 6.08 m] pieces with scenes from the Roman Empire). Use these ideas to create an Oriental rug design for your home, a rug design (tapestry) depicting an event from history and a design highlighting some event in your life. If you are attending a religious school, you might want to design a tapestry of importance in your religion. Make your ideas colorful and record descriptive ideas to their right.

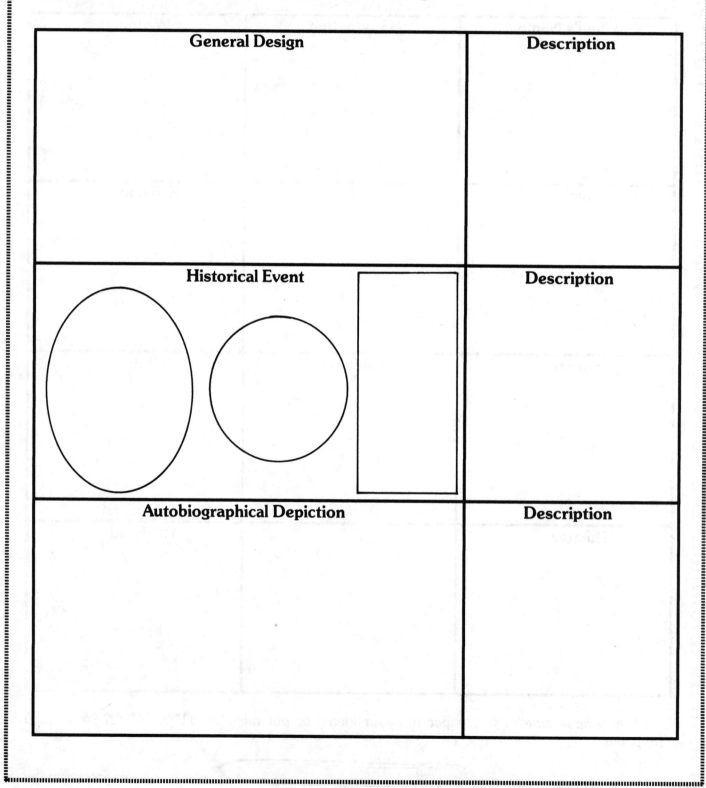

GA1329

Short-Term Projects

You are the head of a baby-sitting agency and have the following business tasks to complete.

1. Insure greater exposure of your business through newspaper, television and radio advertising.
2. Show the public that you offer a variety of baby services other than the straight baby-sitting most people have come to expect.
3. Design a business portfolio and presentation for the local Parent/Teacher Association.
4. Design a speech to convince a local mother/father group that even though you don't use local children, anyone that uses your agency will get caring, personal, reliable and professional assistance.
5. Design a company logo.
6. Create a list of helpful hints for parents using your agency.
7. Create a list of training suggestions for the baby-sitters and professionals you employ.
8. Design an emergency form that parents should keep by the phone for all occasions, not just when there's a baby-sitter.
9. Create a company name and slogan (Grandmother's Hands, etc.).
10. Design a personalized license plate for your own car.
11. Design a new safety feature for the young children business (an impossible-to-fall-out-of crib).
12. Write a speech that the baby-sitter can give to five or six-year-old children that would explain the baby-sitter's job to them and at the same time make them comfortable with the sitter.
13. Design a tricks-up-your-sleeve book that all baby-sitters could use for those difficult and unavoidable situations . . . monster kids, too.

Pick four activities you wish to pursue. Place their numbers in the following space: _____
Preplan your tasks, bounce your ideas off a classmate, use creative and colorful ideas for your projects, form a team and divide the projects between you. Your teacher might want to give one task a day and have everyone work on that particular task. What else would your company need?

The World of Missing Spaces
Drills for Skills I

Every other letter is given for the last names of the famous people listed below. Determine what letter should be placed on each blank to complete the name.

1. ___ L ___ O ___ A ___ R ___
2. ___ I ___ O ___
3. ___ O ___ N ___
4. ___ I ___ C ___ E ___
5. ___ R ___ N ___ L ___ N
6. ___ E ___ E ___ E
7. ___ U ___ M ___ N
8. ___ I ___ E ___ H ___ W ___ R

9. ___ R ___ M ___ N
10. ___ I ___ C ___ L ___
11. ___ O ___ U ___ B ___ S
12. ___ A ___ S ___ R
13. ___ E ___ C ___ L ___ S
14. ___ O ___ S
15. ___ I ___ D ___ E ___ G ___
16. ___ A ___ H ___ R ___

Can you find two common words that will solve each blank puzzle below?

1. ___ T ___ P
2. ___ C ___ O ___ L
3. ___ I ___ Y
4. ___ L ___ S ___

5. ___ T ___ A ___
6. ___ P ___ N
7. ___ R ___ D ___
8. ___ L ___ O ___

You are to place the same number in each blank below. When you add the numbers in the blanks and the numbers already given, your numbers will total the number given.

a. ___ 6 ___ 7 ___ 2 ___ 4 = 27
b. ___ 11 ___ 13 ___ 15 ___ 17 = 100
c. ___ 9 ___ 13 ___ 10 ___ 3 = 50
d. ___ 2 ___ 3 ___ 4 ___ 5 = 31

e. ___ 1 ___ 2 ___ 3 ___ 4 = 58
f. ___ 3 ___ 3 ___ 5 ___ 9 = 100
g. ___ 37 ___ 16 ___ 17 = 109
h. ___ 8 ___ 2 ___ 6 ___ 4 = 56

Write your five best fill-in-the-blank favorite people below. Challenge a classmate to decipher your work.

1. _____
2. _____
3. _____
4. _____
5. _____

ooo best fill·in·the·blank ooo

82

Critical and Creative Prefix Thinking
Drills for Skills II

Place a prefix on the blank in front of the three words given. If you combine the prefix with each given word, you create three new words each starting with the prefix you put on the first line.

Prefix Answer	Word I	Word II	Word III
Ex: micro	wave	scope	film
1. _____	port	turn	cite
2. _____	stance	marine	due
3. _____	vent	jury	form
4. _____	take	chief	tress
5. _____	face	pare	sent
6. _____	cave	done	fine
7. _____	patient	prove	port
8. _____	ma	fort	mend
9. _____	sense	stop	combustible
10. _____	body	septic	aircraft
11. _____	pod	angle	cycle
12. _____	life	get	night

Try this same activity using additional prefixes or suffixes. Prepare ten without answers and exchange them with a classmate. Try this using compound words. Pick three words that would follow the word *house* or *fly*. After the three words are picked, present them to a classmate without the key word.

1. _____   _____   _____   _____
2. _____   _____   _____   _____
3. _____   _____   _____   _____
4. _____   _____   _____   _____
5. _____   _____   _____   _____
6. _____   _____   _____   _____
7. _____   _____   _____   _____
8. _____   _____   _____   _____
9. _____   _____   _____   _____
10. _____   _____   _____   _____

GA1329

Research Suggestions

1. What are the ingredients for dog food? Are horses really used for dog meat? Research these two questions while trying to put together the ideal meal package for a dog. Discuss the various food groups a dog should eat and how he/she benefits from each.

2. Design a poster/advertising campaign for a dog boarding and grooming business. Contact five kennels and compare their rates for overnight boarding, weekly boarding and general grooming and dog care. Make a creative chart of your findings.

3. Design five themes for a school dance. Have the first four correspond to the seasons (four seasonal selections) and the last to a big ball or prom.

4. Design a dateless dance (no couples) where everyone can attend. Design activities that will make everyone a part of the dance.

5. Create a song that would be played by Stan's doggy wagon as it rolled through your community.

6. Invent a baby-sitting robot. Illustrate its physical features and list its one-of-a-kind attributes. Be sure to list the services it performs and the price range for these and any extras you can add. Where will this robot be sold? To-and-from job handling must also be solved.

7. The rug business has worked for years on developing stain and wear resistant fibers. See what you can discover about their work and the history, say for the last fifty years, as to what was used in carpeting. Get a booklet of rug swatches and give a presentation to your class as to why they should cover their classroom with your product. Add new features to your carpet like TV, radio and computer hookups in the carpet layers to encourage people to buy your product.

8. Design a nonthreatening form that a baby-sitter could give to a family with comments about child behavior and general ideas to improve baby-sitting (emergency numbers).

9. What new features would you add to the telephone to make life easier for everyone, especially the handicapped?

10. Research what year it is on three different calendars (Chinese, Jewish, Roman) and give the significance of each.

11. Make a list of five delivery services that a sixteen-year-old might research for employment. List their hourly and weekly wages. Record any additional benefits and avenues for promotion that should also be considered.

GA1329

Teacher Suggestions

1. Discuss the use of dating hot lines (very expensive) and dating services with your class. List the pros and cons of each. Discuss how these services can be improved and make your class aware of the pitfalls.

2. Make a list of telephone and dating conversation icebreakers for people of all ages with your students. Include a list of things not to say, also.

3. Discuss changing date etiquette with your students.

4. Research the history of cars from the Model T to cars of the future. Each of the U.S., as well as the foreign, car makers are anxious to send you pages of information that you can share with your class. Have three local car dealers come in to introduce their new cars and the art of salesmanship. Also, ask them to discuss the other jobs in a car business that might not be as visible as a salesperson or mechanic. Have them explain the commission and salary systems that their companies use. Some salesmen or dealer owners may also be able to discuss starting a franchise.

5. Contact your local Better Business Bureau or chamber of commerce to secure a speaker to talk about small business opportunities and franchises. Most colleges have speakers in these areas, too.

6. Have your class write on the theme My Worst Baby-Sitting Nightmare and then with your students create a booklet on baby-sitting tips we all should know.

7. Talk to your students about designing the locker of the future for their school hallway or athletic locker room. One of the best ideas presented in my class was a sock and sneaker dehumidifier for the smelliest of problems. Have each student illustrate and describe his/ her new product.

8. Start a classroom baby-sitting club where some of the money earned is used to buy that personal computer your class has wanted.

9. Ask a local florist to present all the aspects of the flower business to class. Ask him/her to recommend someone that could follow the lesson with how to make floral arrangements and designs. Then follow this with a landscaper. Remind the florist to discuss what the color of each flower means, in addition to the type and hardiness of various flowers.

10. Have three different restaurant owners give presentations to your class on ethnic foods, cooking schools, the restaurant business, buying meats and other produce, and employee expectations.

GA1329

Write Like a Master I

The theme for the three story starters below is a telephone call. You are encouraged to write only one side of the conversation and try to make the reading audience know exactly what the other person on the phone is explaining to you or discussing. Most of your writing should be centered around the telephone, though you may leave the telephone if you have a creative branch off idea.

Story Starter I

The golden shopping spree? This can't be true. Are you sure you have the right (place your name here) _____? There must be some mistake. I live for shopping. My mother and father tell people my middle name is Mall. Now I have fifteen minutes to "shop til I drop . . . ."

_____

_____

_____

_____

Story Starter II

Come on, phone, ring! Just one little ring from my favorite person. The waiting is killing me. Is it possible to mind meld with someone and will them into calling you? If it happened, I'd probably be scared to death with my new power. How about some secret words from Merlin the Magician or the oracle of Delphi? Don't tell anyone, but my father rubs the cat's back for luck. Only problem is I can't find the cat, and I'm not very lucky. It's ringing . . . the phone is ringing . . . it worked . . . but which formula is correct? Hello, Barton residence . . . .

_____

_____

_____

_____

Story Starter III

What kind of strategy can I use to be the hundredth caller in the Win $10,000 at WWBC Radio's Giveaway? Will it be just luck if I win, or can you time it to be the exact caller? Last night practice showed me that it takes three seconds to hit the button and say, "You are caller #5," etc. Three hundred seconds is exactly five minutes. What if the DJ takes a few deep breaths. No one can just answer the phone for five minutes. Thirty-second leeway. That should do it. The contest starts at ten o'clock. I'll place my call at 10:05 and thirty seconds. 10:05:28, 10:05:29, instant dial activated. It's ringing. "You are caller # . . . ." _____

_____

_____

_____

_____

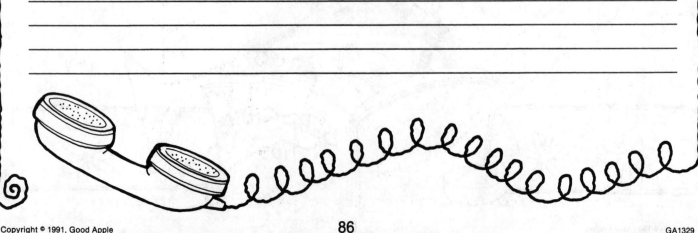

86

GA1329

Write Like a Master II

You might want to try to develop one or two of the themes below in your writing journal. Experiment with writing humorous themes, writing in the first and second person, using a flashback in your story or looking back on an event years after it happened.

Themes

1. He/She stepped on my toes and had a runny nose, but we fell in love anyway.
2. Read Kurt Vonnegut's "Long Walk to Forever" in *Literary Cavalcade* and then write your own "Long Walk to Forever" story.
3. I traded in my six-guns for a wonderful partner.
4. Red convertibles are not the answer.
5. Why didn't they tell me?
6. The single person's guide to combatting loneliness.
7. If Dad/Mom were here, this is what I'd tell him/her about his/her son/daughter.
8. I should have taken lessons.
9. Baby-sitting is for the birds.
10. A torn photograph is my only reminder.
11. Summertime memories
12. My heartstrings can stand the pain.
13. Why I'm not perfect.
14. Parents are smarter than we think.
15. I'll never do these things when I'm a parent.
16. This story never will make *Reader's Digest*.
17. First date jitters
18. Handicapped but not forgotten
19. The world's best baby
20. The world's worst job is mine.
21. I wish you health.

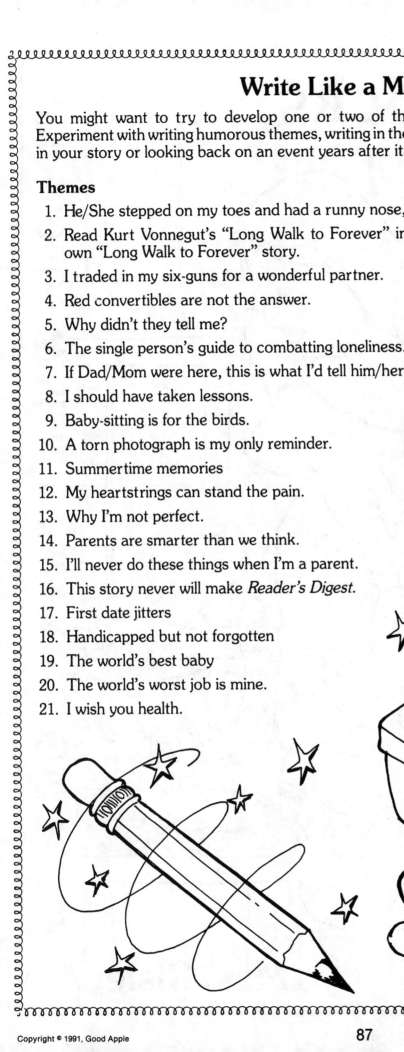

Socks

Kittens for Sale

Lap Sitting

Jealousy

Baby Formula

KITTY

BABY FORMULA

Please By Buy My Kittens

A New Baby William

Fat Kitty

Old Taylor

Mrs. Risley

I thought the same thing you did when your teacher said the title of this week's book is *Socks*. Why would anyone write a book about a pair of socks? Unless maybe they were magical socks. That would be neat-o! Each time the lead characters put on the magical socks, they are transported to some place in time or some vacation spot miles away from home. My second guess was that the socks kept on being passed from interesting person to interesting person until they were too worn to be used. Then a fairy godmother, because the socks had served so many people so well, made them brand-new again. As usual, I was wrong, but my ideas are almost as special as the story about Socks the cat that you are about to read. Socks liked attention. Lack of attention and a small nip of his owner's leg made for some new experiences.

1. Think of three things that make cats lovable and three things that cats do that annoy their owners. Place them in your notebook. After reading *Socks*, see how many of the things you selected appeared in the story.

2. Make a prediction as to the number of parents in your classroom that owned cats before they had children. Of those families that have cats and kids, see who came first.

3. How can you be sure that animals do or do not have feelings?

4. What do you do when you think someone is getting more attention than you are?

5. Cats are generally playful. What objects would be playthings for a cat in a story that you wrote? See how your objects compare to the authors.

6. If you were baby-sitting for a family, would you be bothered by the presence of a cat or dog, even if the dog were really, really big?

7. Name the five best sleeping places for a cat; then name the five most unusual places that cats sleep? (on top of a car's hood).

8. How many foods can you name that come in "light" varieties? Did you ever hear about light foods for dogs and cats? What do these offer that is different from normal cat and dog food?

9. What types of special skills do veterinarians need to know about the care of cats?

10. What special relationship might develop between a baby and a cat?

GA1329

Vowel-itile Sentences
Vexing Vocabulary

strained	garlic	fortunate
exercise	sharpened	instincts
cereal	custard	nuisance
fragrance	simmering	aerial
reproach	anxiously	upholstery
burped	astonishment	contentment
exhausted	possessed	glossy
whiskers	perfect	charming

Ten easy-to-read vowel-less or "missing sentences" are written for you below. Please replace the vowels and list your answer underneath each missing sentence. For this activity, *Y* and *W* are not considered vowels even when they act the part in the sentences you will try to decode.

1. Y CN LK BT DNT CM T CLS.

_____

2. H DVNCD, STLL HSSNG, THRGH TH RN.

_____

3. WHVR HRD F FRSH KTTNS?

_____

4. H WS FSCNTD ND FRGHTND.

_____

5. R Y SR XRCS S PRFCT FR TH HRT?

_____

6. WH CSD LL TH TRBL, SCKS R TH LTTL BBY WLLM?

_____

7. W CNT LT HNDSM BY GT FT, CN W?

_____

8. N YNG PSTRT WS GNG T TLL HM NYTHNG.

_____

9. WTH HS TL DRPNG, RBSY LKD RND.

_____

10. H DD NT HV T MND HS MTHR.

_____

Design five missing vowel sentences using facts from the story. Have a friend decode them.

1. _____
2. _____
3. _____
4. _____
5. _____

GA1329

Just the Facts

1. Who called Socks Skeezix? _____

2. Socks was sold by _____ and _____.

3. What kind of car did the Brickers own? _____

4. Without _____ Socks was bewildered and dejected.

5. Before the baby came, what was Socks rival for Mrs. Bricker's attention? _____

6. Socks felt half a _____ was better than none.

7. Who was Tiffy? _____

8. What was the one comfort in Socks' turned-around world? _____

9. How old is cousin Mike? _____

10. What did Aunt Cassie say frightened the baby? _____

11. What kind of diet was suggested for Socks? _____

12. What percent were Socks' kidney pieces cut down? _____

13. Socks, wiener in his mouth, was poked with a _____

14. Where did the Brickers get Mrs. Risley? _____

15. Socks never experienced _____ on his toe.

Please write a question for a classmate about each of the following:

1. Old Taylor

_____

2. Charles William

_____

3. The Brickers

_____

4. The crib

_____

5. Mrs. Risley

_____

GA1329

What Is Your Opinion?

1. Did you think it was strange that kittens were being sold for a quarter or the best offer?
   _____

2. When Debbie called out "fresh kittens," didn't you think this was an unusual way, that would probably work, to draw attention to her kittens?
   _____

3. Who did you think was more logical at the kitten sale, George or Debbie?
   _____

4. What is good "kitten weather"?
   _____

5. Do you think Socks would have managed in the "bad dog" family? Please explain why he would manage and why he might not have managed.
   _____

6. What would living in a mailbox be like? Do you think a creative author could set up a story where an animal character lived in a mailbox? What kind of animals would be good choices for a live-in-a-mailbox story?
   _____

7. Do you think getting a kitten because he'll look good in front of a fireplace is a wise decision?
   _____

8. When the story began, did you think it was going to have Debbie and George as the lead characters or the Brickers?
   _____

9. Did the description of a shabby house lead you to think that Socks would soon be back with George and Debbie?
   _____

10. In your opinion, why didn't Socks like rivals?
    _____

11. What makes kittens so lovable, and why do you think so many people sometimes become more attached to their pets than fellow human beings?
    _____

12. Do you think taking good care of a pet means that that person would care about other things just as carefully?
    _____

13. New babies are naturally disruptive to a household, but the love and warmth they bring far outshadow the little inconveniences. Do you agree or disagree with this statement?
    _____

14. What would indicate to you that animals can sense when their owners feel happy or sad? Please explain.
    _____

15. Why are babies attracted to bright colorful things like scarves or twirling crib birds?
    _____

16. What part of Socks' and Charles William's playfulness amused you the most?
    _____

17. How would you rate Mrs. Bricker as a new mother? Why?
    _____

The Great Cats
Ideas and Illustrations

For many years, cats have been a symbol of strength, power, quickness, good luck and intelligence. From the Great Sphinx of Egypt to the catlike gargoyles on buildings throughout the world, designers have used cats as their theme throughout the ages. Your task after making replicas of the Great Sphinx and the Pyramids of Cheops, a building with a catlike statue in front or gargoyle corners on the roof, is to design four structures where the cat really dominates the theme of your creation. Some ideas have been added below. Complete them and then fire up your own ideas.

The Great Sphinx/Pyramids	Cat Statue	Cat Building Roof
Cat Baby Toy	**Cat Game**	**Cat Vehicle**

GA1329

 # Animal Observation
Short-Term Project

In this activity book you will find activities based on *The Ramona Quimby Diary*. You have a choice of making a make-believe cat diary with illustrations or doing a real animal study and chronicling exactly what your pet is doing each hour in a set period of time. Spaces have been provided for your notes and pictures below. Most college child development and educational psychology courses make you do this with a baby. Pet or human subjects can be used below.

Subject _____

Subject's name _____

Observation setting _____

Time span (fifteen minutes, hourly, etc.) _____

Time/Written Observations	Illustration/Photo
First Hour	
Second Hour	
Third Hour	
Fourth Hour	
Additional Comments	

GA1329

Cat Got Your Tongue?
Drills for Skills I

The word *cat* appears in exact order in a large number of words. Clues are given to help you narrow the choice of possible answers. Place the number of vowels the answer has over the number of total letters in the answer to determine your fraction. *Y* and *W* are not considered vowels for this activity.

Clue	Answer	Fraction
Example: girl's name	Cathy	⅕
1. mustard's friend		
2. major accident		
3. toss a ball		
4. underground tomb		
5. throw about like seeds		
6. a religion		
7. means "hairy cat"		
8. library files		
9. period of rest/holiday		
10. empty like a house		
11. an elegant church		
12. a group of subjects		
13. ancient stone thrower		
14. party food supplier		
15. livestock (cows)		

Can you take the word *rat* and create fifteen words that have *rat* in them in exact order. Place your best five and clues in the blanks provided for you below.

1. _____   _____   _____
2. _____   _____   _____
3. _____   _____   _____
4. _____   _____   _____
5. _____   _____   _____

Cat got your tongue?

95

Walk Down Mountain
Drills for Skills II

Each structure below is a word mountain. The object is to find paths down the mountain. There are many paths, but only a few of them will give you a word when you get to the last level of the mountain. You must use the letter in every box you touch on the way down. You cannot skip any letter that you can't use. If the letter is on your path, you must use it. You can go back up and down if that is necessary to create a larger word. You can also touch two or more letters on the same line if that will also allow you to create a greater-sized word. You can hit a letter twice if that will help, too. A blank master has been provided for you on the next page to create Walk Down Mountain structures of your own. Your score is the total letters found.

Example:

| B |
| E | A |
| E | T | R |

BEE   BEET
BET   BEAT
BAT   BEAR
BAR   BART

28

1.

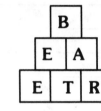

2.

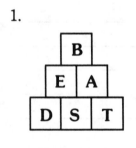

3.

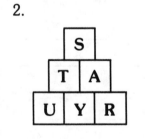

4.

5.

6.

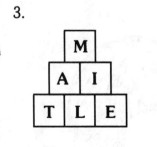

7.

GA1329

Walk Down Mountain
Drills for Skills II—Blank Master

Each structure below is a word mountain. The object is to find paths down the mountain. There are many paths, but only a few of them will give you a word when you get to the last level of the mountain. You must use the letter in every box you touch on the way down. You cannot skip any letter you can't use. If the letter is on your path, you must use it. You can go back up and down if that is necessary to create a larger word. You can also touch two or more letters on the same line if that will also allow you to create a greater-sized word. You can hit a letter twice if that will help, too. This blank master has been provided for you to create Walk Down Mountain structures of your own.

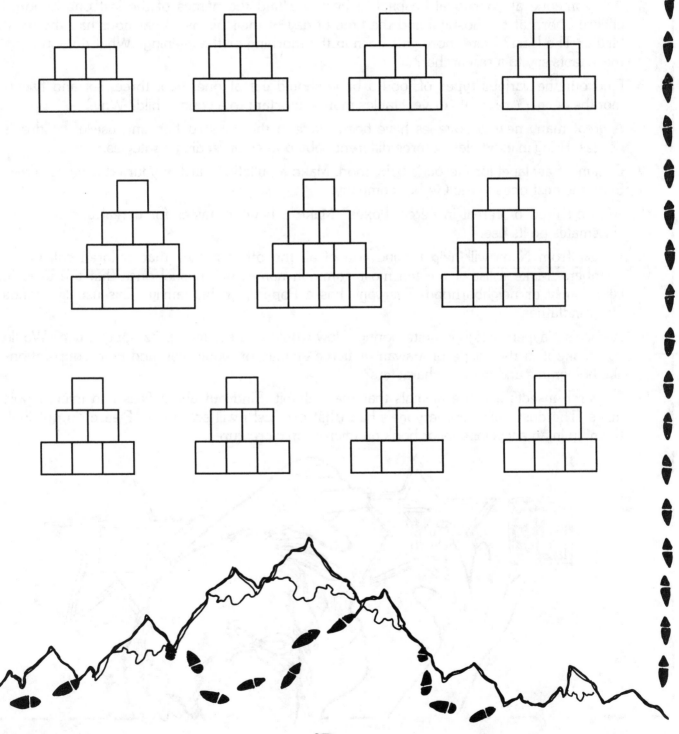

97

GA1329

Research Suggestions

1. Many people say that dog and cat owners look like their pets. Make a make-believe collage of cutouts of famous people. Then use animal cutouts that look like these stars. Place the animal next to the star, so people can see the resemblance. You will find the results humorous and a lot of fun.

2. Compare a puppy's development from birth to six weeks with a baby's development from birth to six weeks. How are they the same? How are they different? How would a cat's development compare to the baby and dog?

3. Find the birth weight of ten members of your class. Rank them in order from smallest to largest. Do the same for baby length. See how the two lists compare.

4. Ask someone at your local hospital to help you find the names of the last one hundred children born at the hospital and the time of day of their births. What hour had the most births? The least? Were more girls born in the morning or the evening? What do you think these facts say to a researcher?

5. Find out the various types of food a baby should eat at one, two, three, six and twelve months of age. Are meats or vegetables more important to a young child? Why?

6. A great many new discoveries have been made in the construction and use of children's bottles. Bring in examples of three different baby bottles or feeding strategies.

7. Design a new label for Gerber's baby food. Make a bulletin board of your classmates' ideas. Send the best ones to the Gerber company.

8. Are you tired of cereal in cereal boxes? Make a new container for cereal and sell your classmates on its use.

9. A visit from Nana will help remind you of all the other names that children call family members. Make a list of the ten most common names or unusual ones that are used in your family or neighborhood. Everyone has a Pop-Pop in his family. This usually stands for grandfather.

10. A child's playpen design is quite boring. How would you spruce up its appearance? Would you make it in the shape of a swan or fierce animal, or would you add neat contraptions like holograms and twirling characters?

11. Research insects and the animals that they inhabit. Find out about fleas and microscopic mites. The dust mites in everyone's bed (that eat flesh) will scare you. Please do not look them up in an encyclopedia or book on microscopic creatures.

98

GA1329

Teacher Suggestions

1. Create a cat-sized mural titled "The Great and Not So Great Cats" with your students. Starting with the eight-inch, four-pound Tabby to twelve-foot, six-hundred-and-sixty-pound Siberian tiger, use transparency paper, poster board and an overhead projector to really make your students' drawings life-like. More and more zoos are building natural habitats for their big cat exhibits. Discuss with your class what is necessary in such a setting. Draw a habitat setting around your cats. Write a local zoo that has a cat habitat for their plans and the feeding habits of the big cats that they have in captivity.

2. We feed our cats and dogs more food than is given to the poor and homeless. Discuss with your class what they think would happen if someone said you can't have dogs and cats anymore. The money you normally would spend on your cat and dog would then be used to eliminate hunger, first in the United States, then in the world. Careful, this is a sensitive topic. But you'll love the points of view of the class.

3. Create a question-of-the-week flip chart. Each week children put their opinions to topical questions, school and community concerns. No thesis is necessary. Just answer yes or no and give a short sentence to back up your choice. My first questions were should children be allowed to chew gum and eat candy in school . . . should animals be used for medical testing . . . what is the best day of the week to test children . . . would you like to be the next person to fly to the moon . . . if you could choose, would you pick a brother or sister for a sibling . . . what time should children (by age) be required to go to bed . . . do you enjoy having your teacher read books to you. . . should McDonald's be given the franchise to run our school lunch program . . . if there were one and only one candy bar in the world, what would you want it to be . . . who would you pick for president or governor? Unique graphing lessons and discussions spring from this simple idea. Other kids from other classrooms even wanted to get their names on the chart to be part of our various surveys.

4. Dear Mom/Dad letters asking for a cat or dog have been a hit at all levels.

5. People who are allergic to cats lead into discussions of other kinds of allergies. Discuss medic alert tags and how to get one with your classroom.

6. The movie *Baby Talk* is good impetus for a classroom writing project. Write as a baby your first day home from the hospital. Comment on your parents' actions and the actions of those around you, pets included. Keep Socks in mind.

7. Have your class parody Shel Silverstein's "One Sister for Sale" with a "One Cat for Sale" poem.

8. Review, then parody, Blake's "Tiger, Tiger Burning Bright" with your children. Kenneth Koch suggests putting a different animal in place of the tiger. Students then complete the poem with the new animal's characteristics.

GA1329

Write Like a Master

The theme of the story starters below is mystery and the unknown mythical/mystical powers of a cat. Review some of the old wives tales about cats sucking away a baby's breath, or being the familiars of witches, before finishing the story starters provided for you.

Story Starter I

Mark, that cat really bothers me. Every time something bad happens, the cat seems to always be on the scene. Is it my imagination or can there possibly be some kind of connection between cats and bad luck? Remember when _____

_____

_____

_____

Story Starter II

I have felt really strange since that cat scratched me. My hearing seems to pick up everything. My vision is ten times better, and my sense of smell has been overwhelming. The dog won't even come near me anymore, and when I put my hand on the fish tank, they all scatter. Could the cat have _____

_____

_____

_____

_____

Story Starter III

This is Commander Bennett of *Moon Base Alpha*. I have a surprise for you, Mission Control. You know those cats you sent up here for weightlessness experimentation? Well, they have somehow opened their cages and are running around on their own. But, that isn't the half of it. They are outside the moonstation without any breathing apparatus. They seem to be ready to _____

_____

_____

_____

Story Starter IV

Bubble, bubble cats are trouble. Make my curse turn those walls into rubble. The castle will soon be mine thanks to my cats and the power of my curse. A few more words and it will fall like an apple from a tree. Power, power _____

_____

_____

_____

_____

GA1329

The Luckiest Girl

Sport Sweaters   San Sebastian

Philip, Jack or Hartley?

Poetry Not Read Well

Journalism Interviews

POETRY READING TONIGHT

SAN SEBASTIAN HIGH

Letters Home

Poor Grades   California or Bust

GA1329

Lead-Ins to Literature

One day Shelley Latham is getting ready for her junior year in school. The next day, she is having a fight with her mother and asks to be shipped to California. Out of the blue, her parents decide a change might be good for Shelley and agree to send her to California. What a break, though some of us wouldn't think leaving our friends, school activities and home in our junior year is the thing to do. Probably if your parents forced you to go, you wouldn't go. In this situation, it was Shelley's choice. Will nine months away be a valuable experience or will it be "unacceptance city"? Read on, surf buddies.

1. What could be worse punishment than being sent to California? Think of some witty remark as an answer to this question that already answered itself.

   _____

2. What kind of disagreement, do you think, precipitated the plea of "Send me to California"?

   _____

3. What three places would you pick for your escape?

   _____

4. Would you send your daughter away for her junior year based on words said in an argument?

   _____

5. Shelley is from Oregon. Do you think she will experience culture shock when she enters school in California?

   _____

6. Would you predict that she will meet friendly people in California or will the author make this move difficult for her, so she will better appreciate what she has at home in Oregon?

   _____

7. Do you think the author will dot the story with trips back home? That way, Shelley will be torn between relationships in both places, or do you think the lead character will be rooted in California to "sink or swim"?

   _____

8. Shelley's mom thinks that sixteen is too young to go to California. She says that Shelley is young for her age. What does this mean, and is it possible to be too young for your age? Please express both points of view in your answer.

   _____

9. What would you concentrate on for your theme in a story titled "Young Girl Goes to California"? Indicate three directions that you would take and then see how close your prediction comes to the actual theme.

   _____

10. What comical situations lend themselves to this young girl in a big state format?

    _____

11. Would you bet Shelley will be happy or sad when she returns home after her nine-month stay in California?

    _____

GA1329

Vexing Vocabulary

linoleum	hamper	relenting
parcel	ingenuity	admission
concise	unanimously	drowsy
gaudy	marveled	argonaut
eucalyptus	admiration	gymnasium
enormous	preferred	episode
diesel	roving	concessions
maneuver	formal	rueful

Because of their multiple and quite different meanings, many words, when taken out of context, give you no clue as to how they were originally intended to be used. Write two sentences for each word below showing two different meanings for each word.

Parcel

1. The parcel of land went for $10,000 at the auction.
2. The post office dropped off a large parcel.

Diesel

1. _____

2. _____

Formal

1. _____

2. _____

Maneuver

1. _____

2. _____

Hamper

1. _____

2. _____

Concession

1. _____

2. _____

Admission

1. _____

2. _____

Episode

1. _____

2. _____

Custom

1. _____

2. _____

GA1329

Just the Facts

1. What is the closest airport to San Sebastian? _____

2. The pink raincoat had a black _____ collar.

3. Oregon's traditional history shows hardy farmers and settlers toiling with their hands to the _____

4. From what kind of wood was Mavis' dining room table made? _____

5. Where did Shelley first meet Philip? _____

6. What category did maidenhair ferns growing along the streams in the woods, trilliums blooming through the last crusts of melting snow in the mountains and dark caves hollowed into the cliffs fall into? _____

7. For a boy, Shelley thought that Hartley was surprisingly easy to _____

8. Where did the countdown to Philip start? _____

9. The nicest party that Shelley ever attended happened on _____

10. Who gave Shelley a *D* in lab? _____

11. What kind of furniture did Pam have in her house? _____

12. What flowers were haunting Shelley less as you progressed through the story? _____

13. Shelley was so homesick she even wrote to _____

14. Who wrote *Litany for a Lizard*? _____

15. What college hosted Jonas Hornbostle? _____

16. The *Argus Report* calls a poet a _____

17. What is the *Bastion*? _____

18. Philip lost his chance to play _____ because of Shelley and his *F* in biology laboratory.

19. The perfume of the _____ _____ grew stronger at night.

20. The letter to Mavis didn't arrive on time because it wasn't sent _____

21. Whose name was written on the head? _____

Who wrote Litany for a Lizard?
THE LUCKIEST GIRL

What Is Your Opinion?

1. Do you believe that leaving home and making a few mistakes is a good way to grow up? Please present your view and the view exactly opposite to yours when answering this statement. _____

_____

2. Would it have mattered if Shelley were in her senior year? Would she have been less likely to leave in that instance . . . missing graduation . . . friends leaving for college, travel and jobs . . . after school weddings, etc. _____

_____

3. Was her escape from home a way to get away from her parents or her friends? _____

4. Do you think picking up and leaving is a way to solve pressing problems? Wouldn't it be better to take them head on? That way, you become stronger with each situation you solve and have "learned ammunition" ready for the next issue/battle/argument/disagreement.

_____

5. What is a girl supposed to do when a boy is shy? _____

_____

6. What is the best and worst "olden time" story that your parents and grandparents tell? _____

7. Shelley was looking for a boyfriend in California, but at the end of the year she was returning to Oregon. Do you think she was being fair to Hartley or anyone else that she would be dating? _____

_____

8. Many people are extremely intelligent about everything after the fact. Do you find that prevalent with the people with whom you discuss important problems, situations and issues?

_____

9. What poet would you interview for a journalism assignment? Please explain why. _____

10. Do you believe in quick or long good-byes in stories? _____

_____

11. The author talks about wanting to hold each hour just a little bit longer. What other things and ideas might we want to hold a little bit longer? _____

_____

GA1329

Movie Casting
Short-Term Project

If you notice the movie credits before a feature begins, you will see the word *casting*. Under it a company like Lynn Stalmaster and Associates usually appears. This company and those like it are responsible for gathering the portfolios of stars, minor players and extras that movie people can use for their next projects. They also gather actors and actresses for television shows, plays, community theaters and a host of other smaller projects. Next to an agent and the jobs that come through their efforts, a casting company listing is an extremely important part of the business.

The form below is your resume and is to be used in the portfolio you have put together with your agent. You can make this a serious/humorous project about yourself, or you can assume the identity of a movie or televison star (Sean Connery, Timothy Dalton, Ben Vereen, Jimmy Smits, Julia Roberts, Cinderella, The Big Bad Wolf) and answer each section as he/she would. Include pictures and cutouts.

Name _____ Stage Name _____

Address _____

Phone _____

Birth date _____ Social Security # _____

Agent's name _____ Company _____

Address _____

Phone _____

College _____

Acting school _____

Studied under _____

Acting Range

_____

_____

_____

_____

Previous Roles

_____

_____

_____

_____

References

_____

_____

_____

GA1329

Movie Ensemble
Short-Term Project II

You work for the Lynn Stalmaster Casting Agency. One of your specialties is bringing book characters to life in movies. You have been asked to put together the portfolios of actors and actresses for a movie called *Sometimes Lucky,* which is based on the Beverly Cleary book *The Luckiest Girl.* What teen and adult stars would you pick for the following roles? Please indicate the last role in which each actor and actress appeared and why you think they are appropriate for the parts indicated.

Shelley Latham should be played by _____

Last role _____

Reason for selection _____

Mrs. Latham should be played by _____

Last role _____

Reason for selection _____

Mr. Latham should be played by _____

Last role _____

Reason for selection _____

Tom should be played by _____

Last role _____

Reason for selection _____

Mavis should be played by _____

Last role _____

Reason for selection _____

Jack (boyfriend 1) should be played by _____

Last role _____

Reason for selection _____

Hartley (boyfriend 2) should be played by _____

Last role _____

Reason for selection _____

Philip (boyfriend 3) should be played by _____

Last role _____

Reason for selection _____

Mr. Ericson (biology teacher) should be played by _____

Last role _____

Reason for selection _____

Katie should be played by _____

Last role _____

Reason for selection _____

Who would you hire for extras and secondary characters? _____

Do you have any portfolios of pets? _____

GA1329

Drills for Skills

Place each column below on an inch-by-inch cube (six cubes in all). The cubes are to be used for the team game on the next page or to see how many of the asked-for outcomes you can get on ten rolls.

Cube 1	Cube 2	Cube 3	Cube 4	Cube 5	Cube 6
we'll	false	out	knock	extra	mist
to	weed	end	hole	part	complete
side	inn	hotel	minute	band	ring
tiny	whole	we'd	back	tune	for
true	out	in	begin	get	melody
half	wheel	real	come	steam	spare

Roll the set five times and record your compound words.

_____   _____   _____
_____   _____   _____

Roll the cubes five times and record your synonyms.

_____   _____   _____

Roll the cubes five times and record your antonyms.

_____   _____   _____
_____   _____   _____

Roll the cubes five times and record your homonyms.

_____   _____   _____
_____   _____   _____

How many words in five rolls can you find that have multiple meanings?

_____   _____   _____
_____   _____   _____

How many long vowel sound words can you generate in five rolls?

_____   _____   _____
_____   _____   _____

How many words with silent letters can you throw in five rolls?

_____   _____   _____
_____   _____   _____

Cube 1 Cube 2 Cube 3 Cube 4 Cube 5 Cube 6

GA1329

In This Corner
Drills for Skills

Below you will find a ten-round boxing match. You can win a round by throwing the least amount of punches. A punch is the roll of the four cubes. You must continue to roll the cubes until you get the desired knockdown. Whoever wins the most rounds is the winner.

Round	Punches		Desired Knockdown
	Boxer 1	Boxer 2	
1.	_____	_____	Roll a compound word
2.	_____	_____	A total of fifteen letters
3.	_____	_____	A synonym (big-large)
4.	_____	_____	An antonym (big-small)
5.	_____	_____	A homonym (two-to)
6.	_____	_____	A contraction
7.	_____	_____	One long vowel word
8.	_____	_____	Two long vowel words
9.	_____	_____	A preposition
10.	_____	_____	*The word *knockout*

Rounds	Won	Totals
Boxer 1		Boxer 2

*Seven-roll limit per round

Round Sums _____ _____

GA1329

Research Suggestions

1. Create three cartoon strips based on the characters in *The Luckiest Girl*. Focus on the situations in the story and then make two spin-off strips based on the events discussed in the book.

2. Write two letters to Dear Abby or Ann Landers using a problem in the story and asking their assistance in solving the problem. Make one request humorous and one serious.

3. Children's literature writers do not dwell on the descriptions of their characters as much as novelists do. Pick three characters from the story and give good physical and background descriptions of them.

4. Imagine that the President is giving a literature award to Beverly Cleary. Write his speech earmarking the things he should say about Beverly Cleary, the love of reading and children's literature in general.

5. Change the setting of *The Luckiest Girl* to another country. What areas would you highlight for the runaway-to town and the hometown? How would the country's location change any of the situations?

6. Create a fifty-dollar-a-day budget for a weekend trip to the beach.

7. Get a catalog from a local college or university and, without hurting anyone's feelings, list what appears to be the three hardest and three easiest courses offered.

8. Review the national and regional weather maps that appear in the daily paper. Design two maps to correspond to the weather you expect for your California weekend.

9. Make a "Great Beaches of the World" poster highlighting the four beaches you would nominate for the best in the world.

10. San Sebastian sounds like a great farm area. Research the California farm industry, irrigation techniques and markets for their products.

11. Make drawings of three different fruit trees highlighting their similarities and differences. "The Great Trees of California's National Parks" is also a good theme for research.

12. You are a lawyer for an underage child who wants to leave home. Write your opening presentation at the court hearing explaining the parameters of the case.

13. Write a "There Is No Place Like Home" poem.

GA1329

Teacher Suggestions

1. Vincente Municipal Airport is hardly discussed in the story. Research with your class the three largest airports in the United States. Then have your class compare these three with the three largest outside of the United States. "Careers in Aviation" is a great topic for an invited classroom guest. We have a "Women in Aviation/Women's Pilot Association" group that does outstanding classroom presentations in the Philadelphia area. Contact your local airport for a list of speakers.

2. Use the thematic approach and have a "Beach Blanket Day" theme. Projects surrounding the day should include.
   a. Design your own beach blanket using old sheets or poster board.
   b. Write a beach poem for admittance to the party.
   c. Famous short stories and movies that incorporate the beach can lead to top tens in books and movies.
   d. Research poems with your class that deal with the beach or stretches of "lone and level sands/the sands of time" that appear in so many descriptive passages.
   e. Write a newspaper story describing the beach volleyball championships, surfing championships or song writing contests held at your particular beach.
   f. Design a miniature surfboard or beach diorama.
   g. Write a convincing essay on "Why Class Should Be Spent at the Beach" detailing the educational benefits that can be derived from beach study. What would the titles of some of your beach courses be?

3. Have your class compare the college study of oceanography with that of biology. Stress the career areas that both of these subjects can prepare students to enter. Research the colleges that have outstanding reputations for study excellence in both of these areas.

4. Discuss the three ways a movie screenplay writer would remake the lead characters to make them stronger personalities on screen.

5. Have a debate on the topic "Why Oregon Is Good for You?" Each member of the debate should present each side of the issue.

6. In literature, the movies and television, who would you say is more often described as more lenient, mothers or dads? Choices should be backed up by specific literature, movie and television references.

7. In Florida you can drive at the age of fourteen. Research the driving and motorbike regulations of your state and those surrounding it. What state has the oldest age for driving? What has the youngest? Reasons?

GA1329

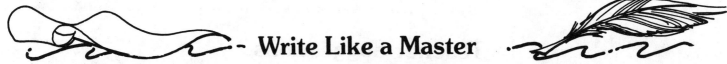

Write Like a Master

The theme of the story starters below is the small talk between a couple on a first date struggling to find conversation topics. You can write both sides of the conversation or write one side as we try to imagine what the silent partner is saying "between the lines."

Story Starter I

Look at that moon! It's so bright that we hardly need streetlights to walk to the theater. Hope the movie is as good as its reviews. If it isn't any good, we can always _____

_____

_____

_____

_____

Story Starter II

This has never happened before. You know what I mean? Since I met you I haven't thought of anything else but this date. I don't have a lot of money, so I planned for us to _____

_____

_____

_____

_____

Story Starter III

I really enjoyed myself tonight. It has been a long time since I had so much fun. I never laughed so hard in my life. Do you write down what you want to say before time? How do you always come up with a funny response? I can't tell when you are serious. Have other girls/boys told you _____

_____

_____

_____

_____

Story Starter IV

Doesn't it seem like the moon is following us? Oh! Don't worry I always take this shortcut through the cemetery to get to the mall. Sure I've taken other people this way and no one ever said a thing. Why would you think this strange when everyone else _____

_____

_____

_____

_____

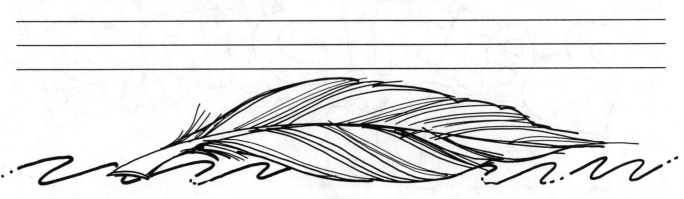

GA1329

Motorcycle Mania

Silly Fights

Ralph S. Mouse

Running the Maze

A Shirt Pocket View

Electronic Mouse Catcher A Crowded Inn

NO MICE WANTED

INN

SCHO

A Trip to School

Friday Exams

Lead-Ins to Literature

Beverly Cleary has written about a dog (Ribsy) and a cat (Socks), so why not include a mouse in your book series? The only problem is that Ralph, the mouse in the story, rides a motorcycle all over the place and travels to school in his best friend's pocket. Maybe Ralph will be some help at spelling test time. No, that would probably be cheating. Follow this intelligent little creature as he tries to get away from pestering mice friends, tries to solve his best friend's quarrels and tries to find someplace he can enjoy riding his motorcycle.

1. As soon as you heard the title, did you ask yourself "I wonder what the *S* in the middle of his name signifies?" Explain your first thoughts upon hearing the title.

   _____

2. Do you think giving an animal character in a story a motorcycle was an excellent way for the author to keep a reader's attention?

   _____

3. What skills and characteristics would you give a mouse in a story? Make a list of your ideas, then predict the ideas Beverly Cleary might use in this story. Make a third list after finishing the story and see which of the first two come closest to it.

   _____

4. If you were snacking while reading *Ralph S. Mouse*, what three foods would be part of your nibbling? If Ralph S. Mouse were reading about you, what do you think he might have for his three snacks?

   _____

5. Look over the book or preview the movie *Mrs. Frisby and the Rats of INMH*, a story about a group of rats that escape from the institute of mental health (INMH) and see if Ralph is a relative. After reading about Ralph, see if you notice any similarities in the two stories.

   _____

6. Can you think of three ways that you can bring a mouse to school without your teacher or classmates' knowledge?

   _____

7. Why do you think Ryan would bring Ralph to school?

   _____

8. Ryan is probably going to get caught with the mouse. What are three excuses he could use for bringing a mouse to school?

   _____

9. Ralph talks, but not everyone hears what he says. What type of person would a good author give the power of hearing and talking with Ralph to?

   _____

10. Would the story be any more interesting if a girl carried Ralph around instead of a boy?

    _____

11. What three additional settings and events would you pick for the story in addition to the school?

    _____

114

Vexing Vocabulary

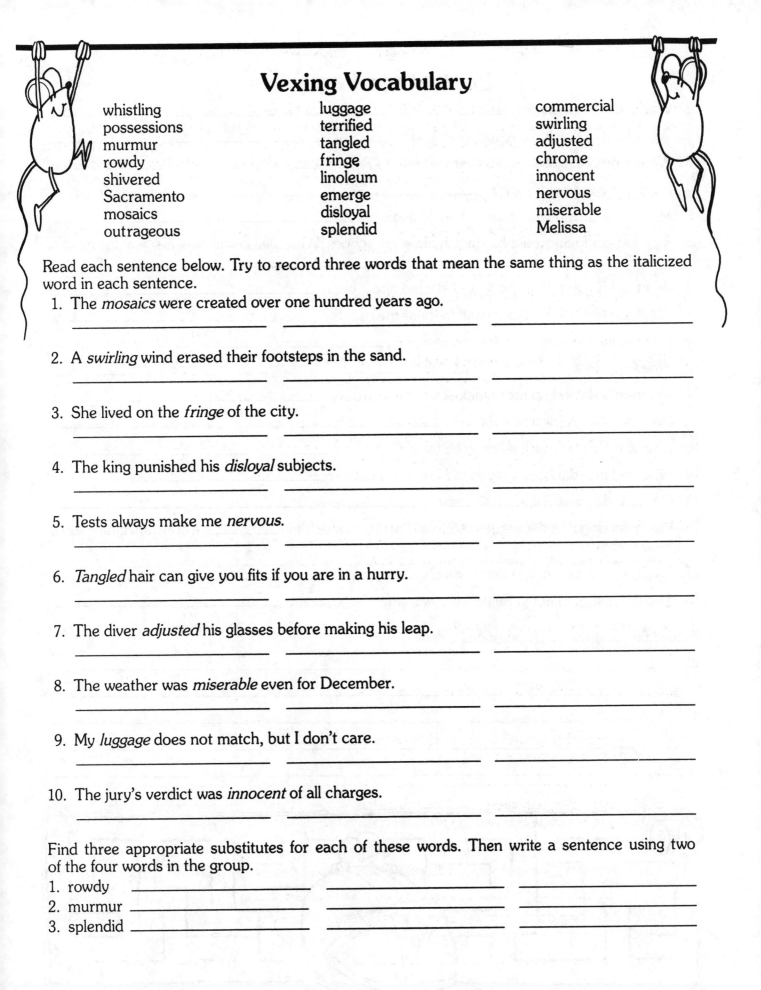

whistling	luggage	commercial
possessions	terrified	swirling
murmur	tangled	adjusted
rowdy	fringe	chrome
shivered	linoleum	innocent
Sacramento	emerge	nervous
mosaics	disloyal	miserable
outrageous	splendid	Melissa

Read each sentence below. Try to record three words that mean the same thing as the italicized word in each sentence.

1. The *mosaics* were created over one hundred years ago.
_____   _____   _____

2. A *swirling* wind erased their footsteps in the sand.
_____   _____   _____

3. She lived on the *fringe* of the city.
_____   _____   _____

4. The king punished his *disloyal* subjects.
_____   _____   _____

5. Tests always make me *nervous*.
_____   _____   _____

6. *Tangled* hair can give you fits if you are in a hurry.
_____   _____   _____

7. The diver *adjusted* his glasses before making his leap.
_____   _____   _____

8. The weather was *miserable* even for December.
_____   _____   _____

9. My *luggage* does not match, but I don't care.
_____   _____   _____

10. The jury's verdict was *innocent* of all charges.
_____   _____   _____

Find three appropriate substitutes for each of these words. Then write a sentence using two of the four words in the group.
1. rowdy _____   _____   _____
2. murmur _____   _____   _____
3. splendid _____   _____   _____

115

GA1329

Just the Facts

1. Where did Ralph live? _____

2. What kind of clock did Ralph sleep under? _____

3. What kind of children could hear and talk to Ralph? _____

4. A rubber band held Ralph's _____ in place.

5. Most of Ralph's relatives knew how to avoid _____ and _____.

6. Ralph knew Ryan would be on schedule for school. What bell count was a signal for Ryan's arrival? _____

7. What did Ralph think moved and started like a bus? _____

8. What caused Ralph to foam and froth at the mouth? _____

9. What state was the locale for this story? _____

10. When was Irwin J. Sneed school built? _____

11. Where did Ralph find his breakfast raisin? _____

12. How did Miss K. describe Ralph? _____

13. How was Ralph's intelligence to be tested? _____

14. What did one dandelion say to the other dandelion? _____

15. On what day was Ralph's maze test? _____

16. Ralph investigated the school and found his back stuck to _____, a substance he hadn't known about.

17. What type of poem did Gloria write? _____

18. The darkest moment in Ralph's life was when his _____.

Record five Just the Facts questions below.

1. _____

2. _____

3. _____

4. _____

5. _____

What Is Your Opinion?

1. The author made only children that were lonely able to hear and talk to Ralph. Would you have included children who were "good of heart" in this category, also? _____
   _____

2. What could you do to jazz up Ralph's home in the clock? _____

3. Ralph was a wizard riding his motorcycle in the hotel, but, don't you think he should have cleaned up the tracks after he was finished? This would be for his safety and would have stopped his friend Matt from getting into trouble. _____
   _____

4. Do you think Ralph's refusal to share his motorcycle with the other mice was mean? _____
   _____
   _____

5. What other alternatives would you suggest to Ralph instead of moving out of the inn? _____
   _____
   _____

6. If you were to build an electronic mouse catcher, what would it include? Where would it be sold? How much would it cost? What kind of guarantee would it carry? Would you design it so it wouldn't kill the mouse? _____
   _____

7. Why do you think a motorcycle-riding mouse is attention getting for young readers? _____
   _____
   _____

8. What other tests in addition to running a maze would you use to test a mouse's intelligence?
   _____
   _____

9. Do you think it was right that Ralph was being used just because Ryan wanted attention?
   _____
   _____

10. How would you have avoided the scuffle that broke Ralph's motorcycle? _____
    _____

11. If you were the author of the story and decided to give Ralph an animal playmate that wasn't a mouse, what kind of animal would you pick? Please explain how you would have this animal interact with Ralph in the story? Maybe you would have Ralph's motorcycle carry a sidecar for the friend. _____
    _____

12. Make a friend suggestion (new character) for Ryan, too.

GA1329

Ideas and Illustrations

After completing the lesson on idioms, see if you can illustrate the three idioms below and then illustrate four idioms of your own. Go on an idiom hunt in a reading book or classroom literature assignment. See how many new idioms you can add to these. Can you imagine how hard it is for a new visitor to the United States to understand half the things we are saying?

1. The crooks had the tables turned on them.
2. He is a real snake in the grass.
3. Day broke in all its glory.
4. The punch rang my bell.
5. He has lost his marbles.
6. They were hot stuff.
7. You scared me right out of my shoes.
8. They were like two peas in a pod.

The punch rang my bell.	The crooks had the tables turned on them.	He is a real snake in the grass.	They were like two peas in a pod.

118

The Mouse Motorcycle Parts Store
Ideas and Illustrations

You are the proud owner of a motorcycle store. The store specializes in parts for motorcycles. A big part of your business is the mouse trade. They love your miniature customized designs for all types of motorcycle accessories. Pictured below are the outlines for a motorcycle jacket, helmet, gas tank, T-shirt, antennae flag, boots, gloves, sidecar and decal. Design each of these the way you think Ralph would want them and then make a second run-through the way you'd want it for your own cycle.

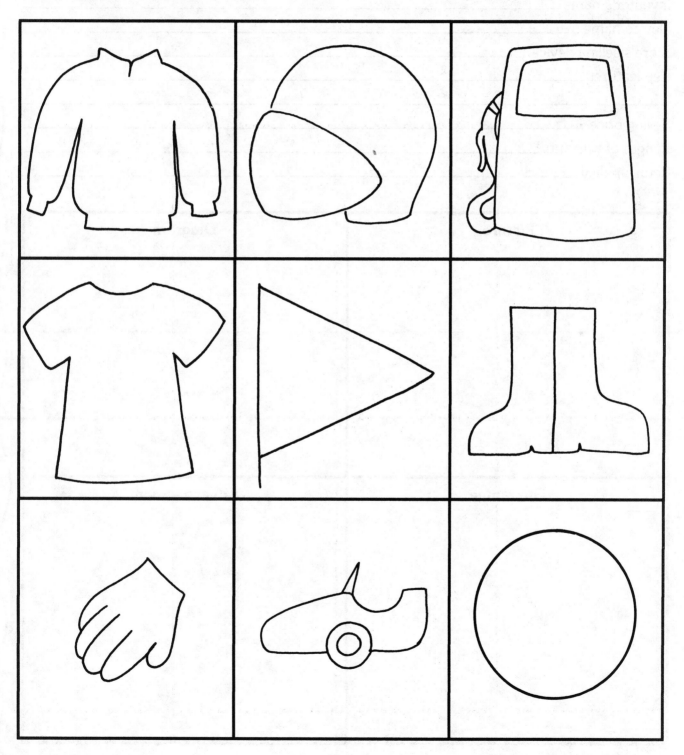

GA1329

The Great Electronic Mouse Catcher
Ideas and Illustrations

Imagine that you are an inventor of a new electronic mousetrap. In the four spaces provided below, draw a picture and diagram of your mousetrap's features. Create a certificate that guarantees its workmanship and results. Design an advertising section of a newspaper announcing your new product and make a cute jingle that would help sell your new device. See if you can come up with a catchy name or phrase that would help you in your promotional campaign.

Inventor's name _____

Device name _____

Store's selling device _____

Key features _____

_____

Selling price _____

Length of warranty _____

Return policy _____

Picture	Diagram
Guarantee	**Advertisement**

GA1329

Short-Term Project

Ralph had difficulty understanding that school didn't move. He heard a conversation about school getting started and figured it was similar to a car getting started. If a car moved after it was started, surely then a school moved. Wrong, Ralph. Imagine what kind of trouble Ralph would have had understanding what these *idioms* mean. After your teacher reviews what an idiom is with your class, pick four of the idioms below and see if you could explain them so even Ralph would understand. You might want to tell how Ralph might get the wrong idea before telling what they really mean. See if you can sneak three of the idioms into your writing assignments throughout the day.

1. Mom has a lead foot.
2. Santa had a twinkle in his eye.
3. Jean has a green thumb.
4. They gave the house a coat of paint.
5. That car was a lemon.
6. The bowler threw a turkey.
7. I'm going to hit the pillow.

8. The report card made him hit the roof.
9. John has butterfingers.
10. Ben was as sharp as a tack.
11. Don't pull my leg.
12. Why don't you go fly a kite.
13. The criminal sang for his supper.
14. He still has one or two tricks up his sleeve.

15. The game is in the bag.
16. Bill cracks me up.
17. The work keeps piling up.
18. That rumor turned into a real snowball.
19. The fighter's manager threw in the towel.
20. His brain is really cooking today.
21. The introduction is a good jumping off point.

22. I will fix his clock.
23. It rained cats and dogs.
24. He is a wise old owl.
25. They turned over a new leaf.
26. She's a real gem.
27. Fred's always crying sour grapes.
28. She's a real blue blood.

29. Gwynn's nose is growing again.
30. Harry is a pain in the neck.
31. Remember, always look before you leap.
32. His words stabbed her in the heart.
33. My stomach is filled with jumping beans.
34. He was left by the side of the road in that deal.
35. How many times did Willie Mays steal home?

The Mice/Mouse Puzzle
Drills for Skills

Each clue below will generate a word that has *ice* or *ouse* in it. These letters appear in exact order in the answer. Your score is determined by multiplying the number of letters in the answer times six or any other value your teacher wishes to have you practice.

Clue	Answer	Score
Example: A living place	house	5 × 6 = 30
1. A small game bird		
2. Salt and pepper		
3. Below president		
4. Rodent/Rodents		
5. Sheriff for one		
6. Cut cheese		
7. Insect		
8. Gondola city		
9. Breakfast drink		
10. Fancy name for *pants*		
11. Follows *twice*		
12. Chocolate dessert (pudding)		
13. Red, black candy sticks		
14. The cost		
15. Secretary's workplace		

Take the *ster* from *hamster* and see how many clues you can give that will create words that have *ster* in them.

1.	Religious holiday	Easter
2.	Word with silver	sterling
3.		
4.		
5.		
6.		
7.		

Research Suggestions

1. Running a maze is an important part of Ralph's story. See what you can find out about the types of mazes used in intelligence testing of humans and animals.

2. Research the story of the minotaur and how its maze was central to the theme of the story. Compare the minotaur's story to that of Alice in *Alice's Adventures in Wonderland* who was in effect lost in a maze of tunnels and experiences.

3. Organize a bike ride-a-thon for the March of Dimes, a local children's hospital or the homeless. Collect money for each mile ridden or lap completed around your track or ball field.

4. Disney World/Land is the largest tourist attraction in the United States. Can you find out what four attractions follow it in the list of places most visited? Have your classmates pick ten sites in the United States and research how many people visit each location in a year's time.

5. Write the state tourist agency in your state and four surrounding states. Ask them to send you vacation and tourist attraction information. If everyone in your class writes to four states, you will have an amazing amount of material for your class research center. Compare the information that each state sends you. Grade each state's information and then pick the best four as to the quality of information they gave you and your classmates.

6. Make a design for a Mouse City. Be sure to explain your plans clearly. Have an overall goal that you want to reach with your new creation.

7. Imagine that you are a doctor at a mouse hospital. What kind of ailments would your mice friends bring to you? Which of these is your specialty? Design your mouse doctor certificate.

8. Take a baseball card (not a Hank Aaron or Mickey Mantle, please) and substitute an animal picture where the ball player should be. Design a Ralph S. Mouse all-star card of motorcycle racing. Try doing the same thing with a Batman or Hulk Hogan card. Make a bulletin board of the best card designs of the class.

9. We are slowly entering the age of robotics. See if you can find a good article on robotics to share with your class. Find out the industries that already use some form of robotics—car industry, dangerous substance industry, etc.

10. Make a list of the top ten animal stories that you have read. If an animal Academy Award was given, what three animals would receive your nomination?

Teacher Suggestions

Make a survey with your class of the types of lodging you have in your area. Have them research the rates for a single/double room, room service, food, phone, cable TV, free lodging for children and the type of credit cards each accepts. This is a great classification activity with all types of spin-offs.

a. Find the hotel with the largest capacity in rooms; then make a comparison of the next nine largest. Make a difference column, so if hotel one has three hundred people and hotel two holds two hundred and seventy-five, the difference column would read twenty-five. Complete this column comparing each hotel to the largest one as well as the one just ahead of yours in size (two subtraction problems). This is needed in case you want to add rooms and move up in the directory of local hotels.

b. Research the different ways lodging establishments advertise in your area. Have the children bring in three different types of advertising and discuss why the ad would attract them to that particular chain or local sleep-over.

c. Pick up twenty-five copies of any hotel chain's worldwide directory. There are map reading skills, opinion and critical thinking activities for lodging selection, travel tips and a host of other activities these guides encourage. Have each team plan a trip to a certain area and record their mileage, nearby tourist attractions and expenses for three days. Journal writing about the three days is also a good spin-off.

d. Have your class design an ad campaign for the imaginary lodge that your school owns. Have each student compose a one-minute radio spot for your lodge or a one-minute introduction for the nightclub act that will be appearing at your establishment this week.

e. Discuss travel and the different types of people to expect on a trip. The bed and breakfast experience and small types of places are undergoing a revival in the United States. What type of person would visit a smaller place instead of a large chain? Compare this experience to European travel.

f. How are hotels and inns supplied? Who does their linen? What are the costs of services that all sleep-over places need? There are a host of jobs that few people consider.

g. Have your local hotel manager talk to the class or get a hotel management professor from a local college to come and explain all the things involved in a hotel management degree, little kids' style, please. How about a local chef or cook to address the children.

124

Teacher Suggestions II

1. Mouse, rat, hamster, guinea pig and rodent comparison activities are good jumping into the *Ralph S. Mouse* story activities. Would it have mattered if Ralph were a hamster or a rat? Rodents are used in many stories from Mickey Mouse to *The Rats of INMH*. Discuss their appeal with the class.

2. Ralph's living in a grandfather clock leads to timepiece research. Have your class create original designs for grandfather clocks, wristwatches and pocket watches with pictures opposite when opened. Going Cuckoo with Cuckoo Clocks is another of my weird theme days. Children must bring in model clocks that they make where something jumps out or tolls the hour. Philadelphia has a famous clock at city hall. Bring in pictures of creative clocks from around the world to show your students. Hopefully, there is a clock collector in your area. Many are creative marvels.

3. Animal intelligence testing and how animals adapt to their environment are big subjects at most colleges. (A mouse's whiskers stop it from banging into things in the dark.) College speakers offer a good variety of topics, even on mice, for young children.

4. Research what rodents are on the endangered species list. Were there any prehistoric creatures that resemble the mouse? Like roaches, they seem to be everywhere, despite efforts to lower their population. What features protect this creature?

5. Have a Happy Birthday, Mickey Mouse party where everyone has to dress up as his/her favorite Disney character.

6. Have the kids imagine a school for mice that Ralph would enjoy attending. Plan a schedule of courses that a mouse might take. Don't forget the mouse lunch menu and recess activities.

   9:00-9:30 Catology: Today's topic is "Can the Cat Be Your Friend?"

   9:30-10:00 Cheese Facts: Today's topic is "Cheese Substitutes."

   10:00 Recess Topic: "Getting the Most Out of Your Spinning Wheel."

7. Have the class discuss the toys that they use with their animals. What three new toys would you recommend for Ralph?

8. Have the class write headlines and newspaper articles about their motorcycle-riding mice.

Write Like a Master

The theme for the story starters below is the tough decision of leaving home. Ralph's decision to just pick up and leave the inn for school was a tough one. Try to make your writing reflect how difficult some decisions can be.

Story Starter I

I know I have to leave, but how do I tell them that it's not because I'm unhappy here? It's just that _____

_____

_____

_____

Story Starter II

My bags are packed. The good-byes have been said. Now if my feet will only leave. Ten years of memories isn't something you just walk away from. My body says go, but my mind has this little red flag sticking up in it. Why is it cautioning me? Everything in my decision seemed logical. The pluses and minuses were weighed and _____

_____

_____

_____

Story Starter III

This hotel is hardly fit for a mouse of my ability. Mice are used to luxury and the finest food, especially gourmet cheese from Wisconsin. That's where I'll take my family—Wisconsin. My travel agent will know_____

_____

_____

_____

Story Starter IV

I am not going and there is no way that they can make me. No one considered my feelings in this move. What about my friends? How will I keep in touch with Latoya from so far away? What about my schoolwork and sports' honors. I'll have to start my life all over again. I like my life the way it is right now. I am just going to tell them _____

_____

_____

_____

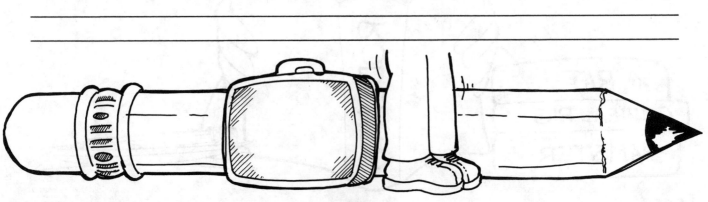

GA1329

Sister of the Bride

Tootie's Trombone   San Francisco

Wedding Plans

Just Cookies

Parental Advice

Traditional vs. Modern

WEDDING DIARY

JUST MARRIED

Grandma's Veil   Bridal Bouquet

GA1329

Lead-Ins to Literature

Weddings are joyous times. They are filled with all types of new ideas and experiences. There is the decision of whether it should be a modern or traditional wedding. Will it be a small wedding or a large one? What to wear? Should the reception be indoors or outdoors? Even the musical group selection has to be made months ahead of time. In *Sister of the Bride*, you will join Barbara Maclane as she helps with and sometimes stays out of the way of her sister's wedding announcement, wedding planning and wedding. From sibling rivalry to boyfriend hunting to growing up to goofy brothers, you will become part of a story that could happen to any of us.

1. What type of wedding do you think Rosemary Maclane will decide on having, modern or traditional?

   _____

2. Do you think wedding selection differs from those living in a small town or large city?

   _____

3. What feelings would you predict the author will discuss as a younger sister watches her older sister prepare to get married?

   _____

4. Since parents have already been through wedding preparations of their own, do you think their ideas will be followed or replaced by differing ones?

   _____

5. Television situation comedies always contain the wisecracking brother. What type of characteristic would you weave into a younger brother in a wedding preparation story?

   _____

6. What other types of situations would you have cross wedding plans that have nothing to do with the wedding theme, yet won't take you too far from the central format . . . lost dog . . . stolen for sale sign . . . new boyfriends/girlfriends for the other brothers and sisters in the house . . . a fire . . . job troubles . . . embarrassing friends . . . super car . . . long lost in-law?

   _____

7. What situations would you place in the story that when read thirty years later would still be ideas that the reader can relate to his/her times?

   _____

8. This story has the older sister being married first. How would the theme change if a younger sister were married first?

   _____

9. What personality would you give the strangest member of the family?

   _____

10. Marriage may not be for everyone. Do you think this story will have a happy ending? If it has a sad ending, how do you think it might affect the reader?

    _____

Vexing Vocabulary

stark	psychology	verbatim
flirtatious	reconcile	Pocahontas
Sacagawea	comprehension	indignant
bouquet	flamenco	intuition
Milwaukee	Hiawatha	hypnotized
ignition	casserole	scheme
apparent	career	lingered
sibling	astute	elaborate

Rewrite each sentence below by adding a word before or after each vocabulary word. The word should make the sentence more powerful and descriptive. Don't throw a word in just because it fits.

1. Nakia always had an *astute* outlook concerning her *career* choices.

_____

2. Jerome *lingered* near the oven *hypnotized* by the smell of the *casserole*.

_____

3. The *flirtatious* moves of the *flamenco* dancer *apparently* were just my imagination.

_____

4. The *stark* apartment and her *indignant* attitude led me to believe that this was some type of *elaborate scheme*.

_____

5. Jenny told me *verbatim* how they tried to *reconcile* their differences over the unsigned *bouquet* of flowers.

_____

6. Your lack of *comprehension* is probably what *ignited* the dispute.

_____

7. It is *apparent* that *psychology* is probably your best subject.

_____

After writing your sentences with the add-on words, rewrite the sentences, this time substituting a word for the original vocabulary words. Your final sentences should be more powerful than the original sentences and your add-on sentences.

Little was said in the story about Milwaukee, Sacagawea, Hiawatha, Pocahontas and flamenco dancers. Do some individual research on each and record an *aside* sentence that would fit in the story using a fact from your research about each topic. Would you have stopped anywhere in the story and developed any of the above topics?

1. _____
2. _____
3. _____
4. _____
5. _____

Just the Facts

1. What is the difference in the ages of Rosemary and Barbara Maclane? _____

2. What is the difference in the age of Rosemary and her fiancé? _____

3. Why weren't there any capital letters in *archy and mehitabel*? _____

4. What was Millie's major? _____

5. At the wedding shower, what signified the presence of a bridal shower present? _____

6. How old is Gordy? _____

7. What did Buster almost destroy? _____

8. "A very sensible arrangement" was Mrs. Maclane's description of what situation? _____

9. How many points did Tootie score in the last basketball game? _____

10. Barbara thought that there is one _____ at every wedding.

11. Gordy's trio is playing for what banquet? _____

12. How long had Grandma saved the wedding veil? _____

13. What was Tootie's real name? _____

14. What was the title of Rosemary's term paper? _____

15. Barbara refused to mend Bill's _____.

16. When Barbara first met Bill, what was he driving? _____

17. What instrument did Gordy play? _____

18. What present did Bill give Barbara on their first anniversary? _____

19. What were the elite Roman guards called? _____

20. Rhododendrons were substituted for _____ leaves.

21. What was Rosemary's first shower present? _____

22. What teams were in the baseball discussion? _____

What Is Your Opinion?

1. Would you find it easier telling both parents at once that you are getting married or one at a time?_____

_____

2. What month would you pick for your wedding? Please explain the significance of picking that month. _____

_____

3. What is your opinion of things people tell you you must do because they are tradition? _____

_____

4. Do you think it is appropriate to date two people at the same time as Barbara might do with Bill and Tootie? _____

_____

5. Why do you think Grandmother kept her wedding veil to give to all the daughters and granddaughters? _____

_____

6. Rosemary's new apartment sounded depressing. What would be the first three things that you would do to spruce it up? I hope lining the garbage can is not one of them. _____

_____

7. Do you think not letting anyone in the house when your parents are not home is an old-fashioned idea? Please explain. _____

_____

8. Do you think it's impolite that both families split the cost of a wedding?

_____

9. Engagement rings are beautiful and memorable, but in this case do you think that the money could have been better spent by Greg and Rosemary, especially after the description of the apartment they were landlording? _____

_____

10. Do you think eighteen is too young to get married? _____

_____

11. People always try to make you what they think you should be. This sometimes can put tremendous pressure on a person who really has no inclination to follow the path that these people want. Do you think Tootie was a strong character for resisting the constant pressure of everyone wanting him to play basketball? What three things have you resisted that everyone has wanted you to do? _____

_____

12. How would you completely change Gordy's character if you were writing this story from a different angle? What would your story angle be? _____

_____

13. If you were writing a spin-off book, what direction would it take? What characters would you carry over? _____

_____

14. How would you give this story a comic ending? _____

_____

GA1329

Ideas and Illustrations

The following four items are sitting on a shelf in a bridal shop (serving tray; punch bowl; knife, fork and spoon; glassware). You are to design them with four different patterns that a couple of soon-to-be newlyweds might select. Take a trip to a jewelry store or look at wedding catalogs for creative ideas. Complete each item as a serious silversmith or glass designer. Then turn the paper over and make each design topical but laugh inspiring.

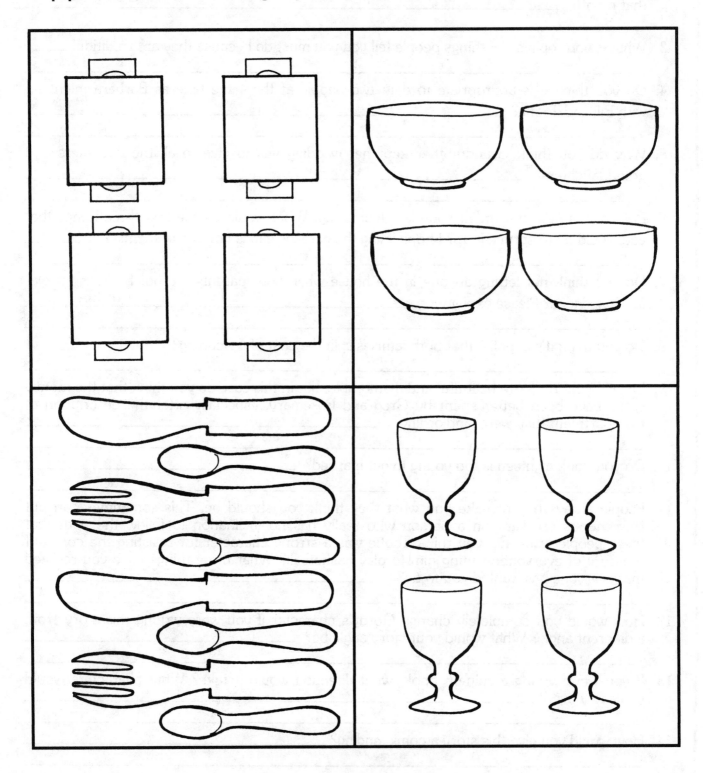

132

Wedding Information Sheet
Short-Term Project

Please complete the information sheet below so an article for our local newspaper can be completed.

Your name _____

Bride's/Groom's name _____

Attending parents _____

Date of wedding _____

Reason date was selected _____

Location of wedding _____

Time of wedding _____

Is there a wedding theme? _____

Wedding march/song " _____ " by _____

Number of members/Names of bridal party

_____

_____

_____

_____

_____

Flower girl's name _____

Ring bearer's name _____

Bride to be given away by _____

Location of the reception _____

Reception band/Performers _____

Toasts to be given by _____ relation _____

Something old, something new worn by bride

_____

_____

Groom's employment _____

Bride's employment _____

Honeymoon destination _____

Bridal showers given by _____

Special guests/Additional newsworthy ideas _____

_____

_____

_____

GA1329

Short-Term Project II

Your creative writing skills will help you as you are asked to compose the following writings and speeches for an upcoming wedding.

Please compose your wedding vows in the space below.

_____
_____
_____
_____

Please compose the minister's charge to the newlyweds.

_____
_____
_____
_____

Wedding dinner toast by _____

_____
_____
_____
_____

Dad's advice to soon-to-be-married son

_____
_____
_____
_____

Mom's advice to a soon-to-be-married daughter

_____
_____
_____
_____

Groom's or bride's words of advice to younger sibling

_____
_____
_____
_____

Younger sibling's best wishes to brother or sister

_____
_____
_____
_____

GA1329

Marriage Survey Graphs
Drills for Skills

Survey three people in your family as to the months of their weddings. Years of their marriages can also be graphed. Combine your findings with your classmates' on the bar graph below. Then take this information and complete three additional graphs using this information. Try not to organize all four graphs in the same order. How about weddings by season or odd and even months (in days) or odd and even years? A tally graph chart has been provided for you to collect the initial information.

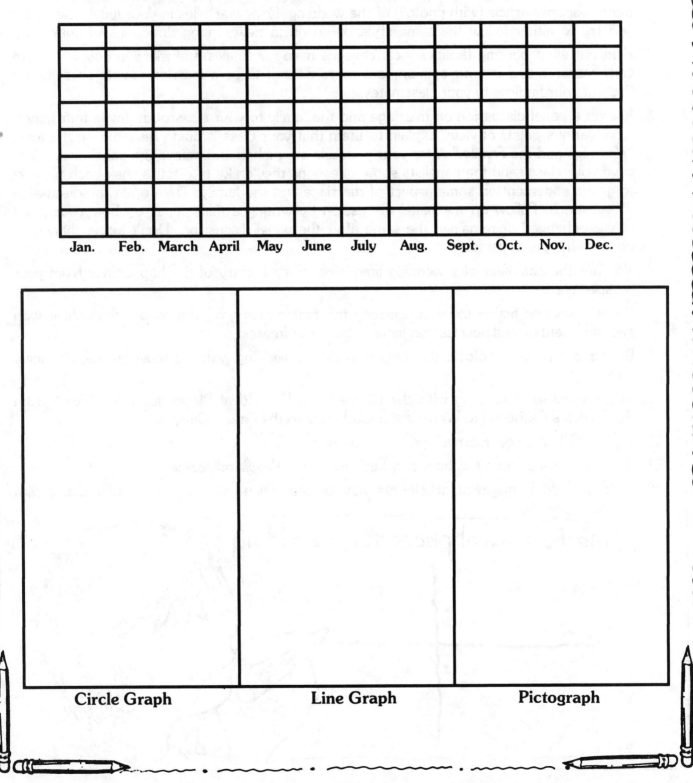

Jan. Feb. March April May June July Aug. Sept. Oct. Nov. Dec.

Circle Graph   Line Graph   Pictograph

Research Suggestions

1. Survey your class with the question what do you think is the ideal age for marriage? Make a bar, line and circle graph with your findings.

2. Plan a traditional wedding on one half of an 11" x 14" (27.94 x 35.56 cm) paper. On the other half, design a "strange but true" wedding presentation. Research out-of-the-ordinary wedding formats (married at home plate in a baseball stadium, while parachuting from a plane, at the bottom of a swimming pool) before designing your attempt at "wedding weirdness."

3. You are a social page reporter. Attend a wedding of someone you do not know. Write the newspaper article (with photo?) of the wedding. Review articles in your local newspaper and try to either follow the same style or go off in new writing directions of your own.

4. Find out what housing facilities local colleges have for singles and married couples. From your research and in your opinion, is it more difficult to be a married couple on campus? Present your findings to your classmates.

5. Recruit a panel discussion on marriage and the family to your classroom. Invite four guests from various points of view. Explain to them that your class is doing research on the topic "Marraige and the Family." After your panelists are picked and before the panel discussion, have your class send the panelists some questions they'd like to discuss. Ask each panelist to give a statement on some aspect of marriage and the family. Then open the discussion to questions. Follow up the panel discussion by writing a mini paper on how your point of view changed or remained the same after the panel discussion. Don't forget thank-you notes to the participants.

6. You are the chauffeur of a wedding limousine. Keep a diary of the happenings from your perspective.

7. Write a science fiction story concerning the first wedding on the moon. Sprinkle it with enough scientific and new fashion facts to keep our interest.

8. Research a record book for the longest wedding, wedding with the most guests, strangest locale, etc.

9. Make a four-part drawing with the theme "The Four Ideal Places for a Wedding" from St. Patrick's Cathedral to Westminster Cathedral to the Grand Canyon.

10. Write a "I'll never get married" poem or limerick.

11. Write a "I was better off without him/her" article for *People* magazine.

12. Write a wedding magazine article/interview of Lady Diana and Prince Charles. Dot it with royalty research.

The four ideal places for a wedding

136

Teacher Suggestions

1. Have your class research the wedding ceremonies of three different religions. Try to pick three religions that aren't the most prevalent in your community. Have the class pay particular significance to the rites, historical background, objects used and special meanings of the service. Then have your class compare these facts to their own religion's ceremony.

2. Compare the cost of three local colleges with three out-of-state colleges. Have each member of your class write to a university for course, fee and enrollment information. Keep a chart of the college's degree programs, scholarship and financial assistance, special programs, aptitude scores needed, campus job opportunities, social and cultural activities, ratio of men to women, graduate placement rates, etc.

3. Write to the Chamber of Commerce of the town where each college and university is located. Also write to the state's or region's vacation bureau for information. Have your students organize and present their findings to their classmates. "Why I think you should choose _____ for college" multimedia presentations are usually great for quality research, idea sharing and humor. If you check every stage, such as, everyone brings their "writing for information" letter to class the same day for language and punctuation assistance and you mail all the completed copies together, you will find answers arriving at about the same time.

4. Have your class design a "college is" mural depicting the benefits of going to college or college life.

5. Have your class design a "there is more to life than college" mural depicting that college does not have to be your only choice after graduation.

6. Have your class design a "see the world before college" mural focusing on choices like travel that are open to graduates before college.

7. Invite a bridal boutique owner to class to discuss the business, fashion design, wedding costs and the job opportunities creative people might want to pursue.

8. Have half the class write "Mom/Dad, I am going to get married" speeches, while the other half of the class writes "Son/Daughter, there is no way you are going to get married" responses.

9. Have your class research "the ideal place for a honeymoon." Presentations should include illustrations, lodging information, facts about the area, sites to see, three-day itinerary, transportation routes from the front of the school and total costs.

GA1329

Write Like a Master

The theme for the story starters below is the indecision that goes through every potential newlywed's mind as to whether or not he/she is making the right decision about this person with whom he/she will be spending the rest of his/her life. Try to make some of your points serious and some humorous. Make your points of what is going through that person's mind believable in both instances.

Story Starter I

Am I crazy? Why ruin a perfectly happy life with marraige? It's not like we are in love. It's just that we can't live without each other. My mind won't let me think of anyone or anything else. Will these feelings last or _____

_____

_____

_____

_____

Story Starter II

Welcome to this marriage and family workshop. I see we have just as many married couples as we do potential newlyweds. As our brochure indicated, today's topics of discussion will cover the following important points: _____

_____

_____

_____

_____

Story Starter III

Sure I believe in love at first sight, even though since the age of two we were destined for each other. A lot of people in love talk this way. What did you expect me to say? That I didn't

_____

_____

_____

_____

Story Starter IV

Look, I told you the wedding is off. They're my family and no one is going to make fun of them. No, it is not "marry me, marry my family." It is just a matter of respect. _____

_____

_____

_____

_____

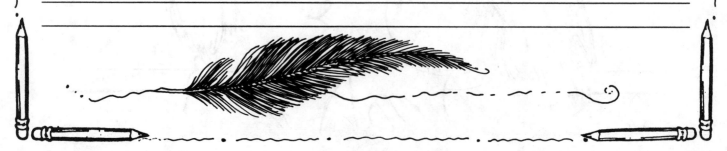

GA1329

Embarrassing Secrets Ballet Class

Ellen Tebbits

Otis Spofford

Fastest Gun in the West

Third Grade Adventures

Horseback Riding

Untied Sash White Horses

Lead-Ins to Literature

Underwear secrets hardly seem like a good topic for a children's literature story. Yet, because of these secrets best friends meet, ballet is introduced and the humorous situations they cause will probably make you giggle and hope they never happen to you. You will also meet Otis Spofford. "Mr. Mischief" will be featured in another book, but you'll get a really good idea of the trouble he can cause as you read this story.

1. I remember the time that my mother put my name in permanent ink on my underwear for camp. I'm standing in the shower and all the kids are laughing at me and pointing. The ink, because of the hot weather, got transferred to my rear end, and it took two days before it would wash off. The kids said it was put there by my mother so I would remember my name. How embarrassing! Can you think of three underwear problems that a child might have in a story like the one about Ellen Tebbits that you are about to read?

   _____

2. What ballet class situations would you put in a story about fourth graders? Eighth graders? Seniors? What situations would be the same for all three groups, and which ones could only pertain to one group?

   _____

3. Otis Spofford is a constant pest to the girls in his class. Try to predict three things that he might pull on Ellen and her friends. See how close you came to the actual events in the story.

   _____

4. Try to picture three things that would happen in a story if you were horseback riding in the city, in the country, on a trail never traveled before.

   _____

5. In this story you will find that Ellen wants to be picked to clap erasers. What kind of positive things would you suggest to Ellen to get her teacher's attention, so she can be picked for eraser clapping?

   _____

6. This is one of the few children's stories where a pet is not involved in the story. Why do you think an author would choose to exclude pets from a story? Don't you think this story would keep your attention longer, if a goofy pet were involved in the action? Do you find that children with pets like to compare their pets with the ones they read about in stories?

   _____

7. Do you ever start a story intending not to like it before starting to read it?

   _____

8. Do you like to read stories where children make their own decisions or where they get good direction from their parents?

   _____

9. Many people don't want to be the boss. Is this a good trait or should we all strive to be the boss?

   _____

UNDERWEAR SECRETS...

140

GA1329

Connect-O-Meanings
Vexing Vocabulary

squatted	taproot	modestly	coughed
hastily	teetery	autumn	bulge
despised	squealed	audience	fault
wade	relief	neighbor	corral
ambled	dismay	biennial	furiously
gnomes	memorize	wistfully	knelt

Connect-O-Meanings are word diagrams that combine a letter in the original vocabulary word with a letter in a word that is similar in meaning. See how many of the twenty-four vocabulary words you can combine in a Connect-O-Meaning diagram. Some have already been completed for you. (These can also be completed with words that are opposite in meaning to the key words.)

```
H                         F                                    C
A                         AUTUMN                               R
T                         L                                    O
E                         L                                    U
DESPISED                                                       C
                                                               H
                                                               E
                                                        SQUATTED
```

AUDIENCE   RELIEF   AMBLED   FURIOUSLY

WISTFULLY   MODESTLY   TEETERY   FAULT

NEIGHBOR   DISMAY   GNOMES   KNELT

MEMORIZE   TAPROOT   HASTILY   BULGE

WADE   CORRAL   COUGHED   B
                                                 I
                                                 E
                                                 N
SQUEALED   N
                                                 I
                                                 A
                                                 L

  GA1329

Just the Facts

1. How many ballet positions were discussed in the story? _____
2. What was Mrs. Spofford's first name? _____
3. The fourth graders were performing what play for Open House? _____
4. Who wanted the "substitute rat"? _____
5. Why wasn't a wide sash right for Austine in the words of her mother? _____
6. How big was the stalk of Ellen's monster beet? _____
7. Where did the "gentle as a kitten" horses once work? _____
8. Otis was told to save his Mexican jumping beans for _____ class.
9. What was used in the bucket to blow soapsud bubbles? _____
10. The material was red and printed with darling little _____ and _____.

Write a series of Just the Facts questions to exchange with a classmate. Use the following situations to create your ideas.

Underwear hiding _____

Otis Spofford _____

Muddy skirts _____

Maypole dancing _____

Best friends _____

California talk _____

Quarrels _____

Eraser cleaning _____

Pretending _____

Alphabet game _____

Zigzag River _____

GA1329

What Is Your Opinion?

1. Why would a good author talk about horseback riding when so few of us have had the opportunity to ride a horse? _____
   _____

2. Most ballet students need to be in better condition than the average football, basketball or baseball player. Do you agree or disagree with this statement? Why? _____
   _____

3. Is there anything likable about Otis Spofford? _____
   _____

4. What do you feel are the dangers and benefits of horseback riding? _____
   _____

5. How do you feel about underwear as a children's story topic? _____
   _____

6. What is the fascination of clapping erasers that so many kids can't wait to volunteer? _____
   _____

7. If you went to dance school, what three dances would you want to learn? _____
   _____

8. Do you think you should enter an activity that you can't possibly be good at doing? Art class, dancing, sports, etc.? _____
   _____

9. Being a rat in a play does not sound like an interesting avocation. Can you think of any animals that you wouldn't mind playing in a classic children's literature story?
   _____

10. Would you rather be good with your hands (art, home repairs, builder) or quick on your feet (dance, sports)? Why? _____
    _____

11. Who is the greatest movie cowboy of all time? Why? _____
    _____

12. Does your school focus enough attention on the art of dance? What would you suggest to increase school involvement in dance, the theater or art? _____
    _____

13. Are more friends made because of common interests or sharing interests that are not the same? _____
    _____

14. Can characters that are pests be liked by book readers? _____
    _____

GA1329

Draw Like a Master
Ideas and Illustrations

Below you will find four scenes from *Ellen Tebbits*. Your job is to make an exact duplicate of each of the four drawings in the space provided next to each drawing. After completing your four drawings, cut them out in a continuous strip. Place your four-part strip next to each of your classmate's strips, and you will make a fascinating bulletin board. Remember to put one copy of the book's strip on each side of your classmate's (25 or so) drawings. The author prefers that the pictures not be colored in. If you like color for the activity, please make it colored pencil only. Wide crayons spoil the similarity in lines that we are striving to achieve.

Master Drawing   **Student Drawing**

144

GA1329

Branding Your Cows and Horses
Short-Term Project

Every ranch in the Old West had a brand that was placed on horses and cattle to easily identify proper ownership. You will find fourteen brand suggestions that the author might use for his imaginary ranch (*T* represents Tom and is easier to work with than a *P*). Please draw the brand that would go with each suggested title. Some have been completed for you. On a new sheet of paper, place ten possible names for your ranch and the drawings of your brands that might go with each one.

Circle T	Rocking Chair T	Box T	Broad T
Split T	River Cross T	Double T	Lassoed T
Bent T	Flying T	Crooked T	Twin T
Bar T	Running T	Leaning T	Triangle T

GA1329

Order of the Rose
Short-Term Project II

Your secret society is called The Royal Order of the Rose. Membership is limited and challenging. Have your classmates select the ten hardest-to-spell flowers. You must be able to spell each before you can be admitted to the order. You must then design an official medallion that is to be worn by each club member. You must also create a personalized club oath and flag. Finally, you must design three good deeds and complete them to gain official membership. Use the spaces below for each of your tasks. Good luck!

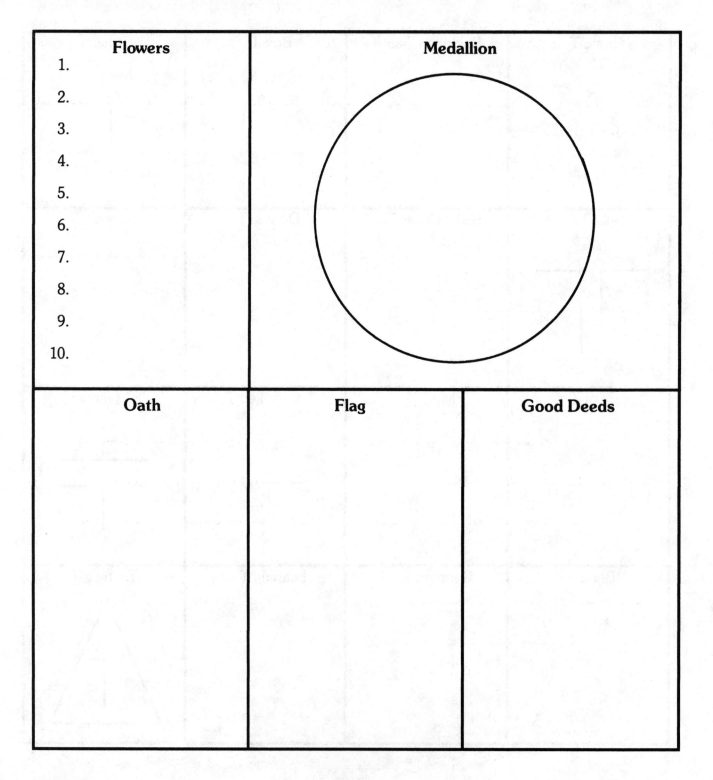

Flowers
1.
2.
3.
4.
5.
6.
7.
8.
9.
10.

Medallion

Oath

Flag

Good Deeds

GA1329

First and Last Word Charts
Drills for Skills
Student Directions

Each chart below has a word written down the left side and repeated across the bottom. The box where the letters would meet is designed to hold words that begin with the letter on the left and end with the letter on the bottom. See if you can complete each chart by finding a word for every situation. This activity can be made extremely difficult by deciding before time that every answer must be a five or six-letter word. The first chart is completed for you and a blank master is provided for you on the next page. Choose a partner and alternate turns selecting a word to put to the left and below each blank chart. Try your name or your school's name for starters.

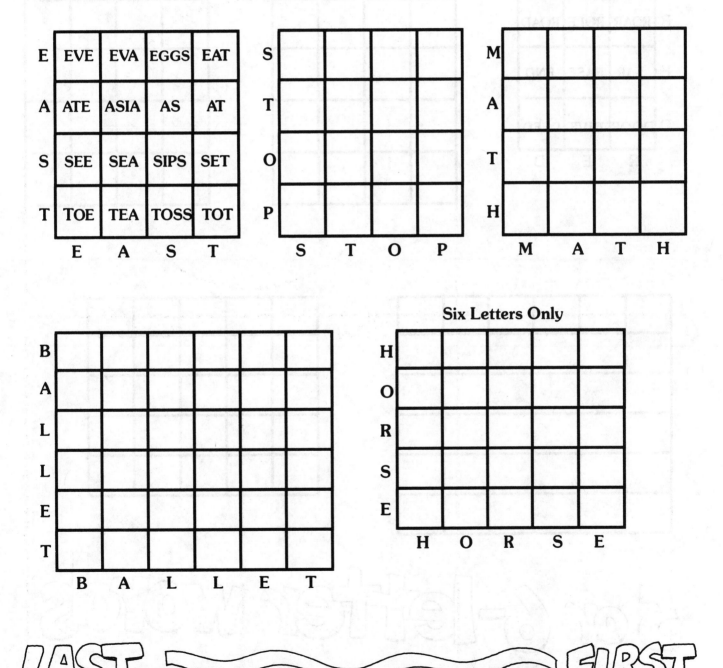

E	EVE	EVA	EGGS	EAT
A	ATE	ASIA	AS	AT
S	SEE	SEA	SIPS	SET
T	TOE	TEA	TOSS	TOT

E   A   S   T

S, T, O, P down / S T O P across

M, A, T, H down / M A T H across

B, A, L, L, E, T down / B A L L E T across

Six Letters Only

H, O, R, S, E down / H O R S E across

GA1329

First and Last Word Charts
Drills for Skills—Blank Master

Each chart below should have a word written down the left side and repeated across the bottom. The box where the letters would meet are designed to hold words that begin with the letter on the left and end with the letter on the bottom. See if you can complete each chart by finding a word for every situation. This activity can be made extremely difficult by deciding before time that every answer must be a five or six-letter word. The first chart is completed for you. Choose a partner and alternate turns selecting a word to put to the left and below each blank chart. Try your name or your school's name for starters.

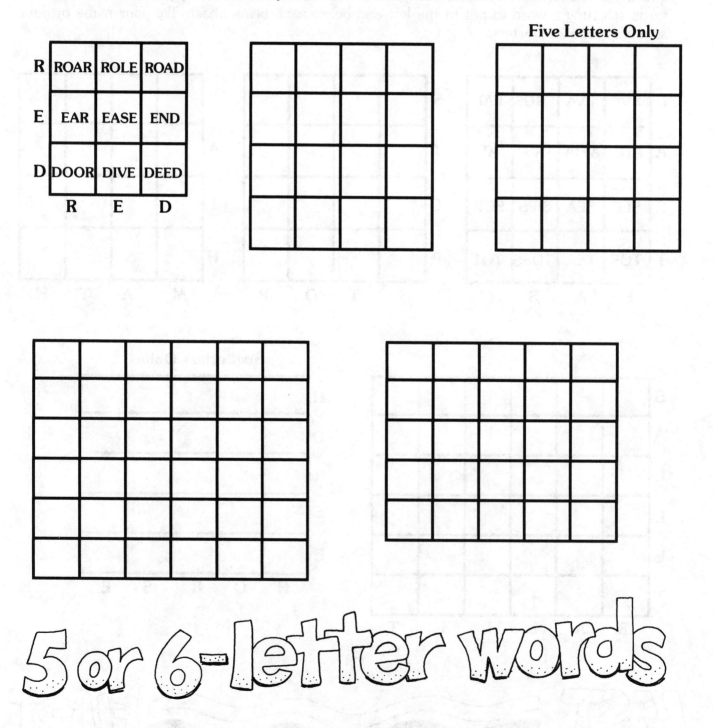

Five Letters Only

	R	E	D
R	ROAR	ROLE	ROAD
E	EAR	EASE	END
D	DOOR	DIVE	DEED

5 or 6-letter words

148

Research Suggestions

1. What can you find out about the various breeds of horses? Illustrate five categories. Read about the history of the horse in North and South America.

2. Horse breeding is a gigantic business. Find out the name of some of the larger farms in Florida, California and Kentucky and write them for breeding information. Find out what stud horses they have available, their backgrounds and costs of service. A local racetrack or stable might also provide you with similar information.

3. Get catalogs from three companies (Sears, L.L. Bean, Macy's, etc.). Cut out their underwear ads and do a little comparison shopping with your recommendations of where to shop for tops, bottoms and accessories in 1, 2, 3 order. Place the companies across the top of a chart. Then downward list ten items that we all purchase. Next to each item in the company column rate them 1, 2, 3 by company. Make sure you have the evidence to back up the choices. Include more than just cost in your evaluation. How about looks and variety of styles?

4. Create a Maypole dance song that would salute spring and welcome the month of May.

5. What type of program could your class organize for a local veterans' hospital? Maybe you could organize a tutoring program where injured veterans could come into your school to work with students in science, geography, history, reading or math. It would benefit both your school and each veteran involved.

6. Create an imaginary campaign to elect Otis Spofford your class president.

7. Create an illustrated dance or horse academy banner or billboard.

8. Create a "friendship is" poem or limerick.

9. Design a "helpful hints in horseback riding" poster that would be on display at the local stable.

10. Make a "I hid in the closet because" list. See if you can jot down ten things that would cause you to hide in the closet.

11. Make a ten-sentence, double synonym listing that follows this pattern: A) That was a beat beet. B) He certainly was a bare bear. C) Our groceries gave us some sum. D) Gene's jeans had holes in the knees. E) Ten o'clock was our hour for tennis. F) The table was for four.

GA1329

Teacher Suggestions

1. The story's discussion of annual and biennial flowers is a good lead-in to the characteristics of flowers. Invite your local flower shop owner to your class to discuss local favorites and the flower business. Have each child sketch the state flower of four states. Below each flower the drawer will give additional information concerning the state's area, population and principal industries. This makes an eye catching and informative bulletin board project.

2. Have your class sketch the five ballet positions and compare their drawings to the works of Degas that can be found in any art book of the period. One third of the class could concentrate on his horse pictures while the other third makes copies of his flower drawings.

3. Discuss with your class why Degas might have made a good illustrator for this book. Have the class select some of his works that would follow the theme of *Ellen Tebbits*.

4. Horses are measured in hands. Have your students work on graphs that would correspond to how many hands high each child in the classroom would be. Circle, bar and pictographs can be used along with actual cut-out hands in strips that will represent each child. Fractions of a hand should also be represented.

5. "Name That Business" activities could include naming a dance studio, horseback riding academy, hair salon and school for potential actors and actresses that would have appeared in this story.

6. Have your class imagine that *Ellen Tebbits* is a new television series. *TV Guide* has asked you to draw the new fall cover and write a short introduction for the new program. Mount the introductions on a bulletin board that has a TV in the middle with *Ellen Tebbits* written on the screen.

7. Discuss with your class why an author like Beverly Cleary would make a new book that also featured Otis Spofford.

8. You are the proud owner of a riding academy. What would a day's schedule of activities look like? Compare the cost of boarding a horse in your area with that of a cat or dog.

9. Make a chart with your class of those activities that you need only one person to do, two people, three people (1—fishing; 2—boxing; 3—bobsledding). See if you can find six activities for each group.

10. Rediscover the art of making papier-mâché masks.

Write Like a Master

The theme of the story starters below is that of magical shoes. Each time the lead character puts on these shoes something quite different from the ordinary happens. Try to think of ten things magical shoes might do before you start writing. Trace with your classmates the properties of shoes that you already know authors have used in stories ranging from the *Wizard of Oz* to *Cinderella*. See if you can create outlines for four books that could be written about the escapades of magical shoes.

Story Starter I

They were sitting on top of the refrigerator at the far end of the junkyard. I don't know why I tried them on. Standing there in shoes too big for me, I started to see the people who had worn these shoes before me. There were three poeple in all. The first owner was a musician. I actually saw the shoes touch the piano pedals. A barber wore them next but most interesting of all was a bus driver who _____

_____

_____

_____

_____

Story Starter II

My father said that his father gave them to him, so he thought it only natural that he give them to me. My father's feet are about three sizes bigger than mine, but when I put the baseball shoes on, they fit perfectly. I played the best game of my life that first night and again for the second game. Now it was the championship game and the rain from the night before shrunk my shoes so I couldn't wear them. There was only one thing left for me to do. I picked the shoes up and _____

_____

_____

_____

_____

Story Starter III

I was the worst dancer in class. When Mrs. Spirow said "Try these shoes; maybe they'll help," I sort of laughed to myself. Nothing will help "Old Two Left Feet." I've banged into more people in class than a demolition derby driver. I couldn't be any worse, so I tried the shoes. Wonder of wonders! When everyone was doing ballet steps, my shoes were doing perfect tap. If I could figure out how to make them do what everyone else was doing, my life would be much more enjoyable. I thought a good idea was to _____

_____

_____

_____

_____

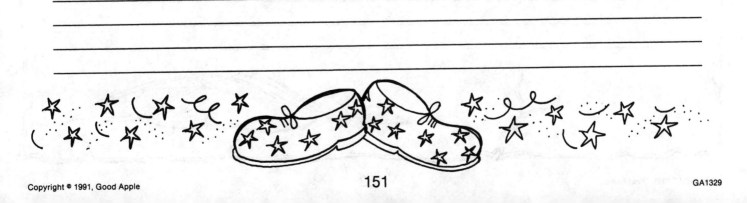

GA1329

Write Like a Master
Additional Suggestions

Here are fifty additional story, writing and idea follow-ups to the "Write Like a Master" sections in each of the Beverly Cleary stories that you have just completed. They should give you a wealth of additional writing formats. These formats are designed to broaden and improve your writing skills. You may continue the starters below or use them as a spin-off for your own ideas. For instance, if you don't like our movie write-up (suggestion #1), you might do a new record, TV show or new book write-up. Follow your teacher's writing assignment directions and clear your new ideas with him/her before taking off on your own. Make your selection. Then try to write four additional lines for each starter on this side of the paper. Turn the paper over to continue your thoughts. Develop one new thought a week.

1. Touchstone Pictures is proud to present Goldie Hawn and Mel Gibson in this summer's most romantic comedy *Kissing Bandits*. You will laugh! You will cry! You will be amazed at the special effects! But most of all, you will never figure out who "dunnit" in this modern mystery _____

_____

_____

_____

2. I never believed in spirits, ghosts or the supernatural until that night we visited the Fitzgerald Mansion. It was boarded closed for years. I thought the stories of strange happenings were just meant to keep people away from the place. Little did I know that _____

_____

_____

3. No one can imagine the death and destruction that an earthquake causes. Bodies were everywhere. Those hospitals that were left standing couldn't handle the onslaught of the injured. The exodus of survivors from the city clogged every transportation artery. The city was without food, water, medicine and electricity. The police _____

_____

_____

_____

4. I saw the body floating facedown in the water. I knew that it was murder, not an accident. A swimming pool would, of course, be the perfect spot to fake an accident. They would have to get up pretty early in the morning to fool ace crime stopper (your name) _____.
Three things gave them away _____

_____

_____

_____

GA1329

5. Jonas Salk cured polio. Marie Curie's discoveries led us to the undiscovered power of uranium and radium. What medical discoveries can a first-year doctor discover? Helping needy patients is important to me, but somehow it doesn't seem like enough. I know that in me and my research is a cure for _____. Ever since _____ I've wanted to find a cure for _____. Now is my chance _____

_____

_____

6. They had grown up next door to each other in a quiet country setting. She was planning to move to the city. He was upset. She never realized that, to him, she was much more than a friend. Their favorite park bench was a perfect place to talk to her. He began _____

_____

_____

7. No one knew how long it was growing, better yet, festering underground. It was far more unspeakable than the horror you read about in books or see in the movies. Grotesque, awkward, but with an unquenchable hunger, it entered the small mountain town of *Poltan*. Its devastating powers seemed unstoppable. There was one last hope _____

_____

_____

_____

8. I was a poor unknown artist. My rent money was running out, and it looked like my canvasses would soon join me out in the street. Sometimes when things look their darkest, a ray of hope appears. My ray of hope was _____

_____

_____

_____

9. That rabbit is driving me crazy. First my carrots, then the lettuce. Elmer Fudd will take no more! My new plan will get that rabbit. First I'll _____

_____

_____

_____

10. The box felt strange. It appeared to be ten times heavier than its size would indicate. The label said "Don't open until the year 2000." That is several years away. Whatever is in the box seems to be telling me to open it now. The "push here" indicator seemed hot, but looked like the spot to start. It was a mistake _____

_____

_____

_____

11. It was a long fly ball hit to deep center field. My legs were moving as fast as they could. I reached out for the ball, and the next thing I knew I was in Yankee stadium standing next to Babe Ruth. I must have run through some kind of time warp _____

_____

_____

_____

12. No one understands how I feel about flowers. They think I'm strange because all my book reports and projects are based on flowers. There is something mysterious about flowers, but that isn't what fascinates me. I just picked a field that I wanted to know more about than anyone else, the world's foremost authority on flowers. You can learn much about life studying flowers. They _____

_____

_____

_____

13. Can video games come to life? "No," you say. How wrong you are _____

_____

_____

_____

14. What was the strangest thing you have ever seen looking out your classroom window? No one in my class believed the things we saw. Lucky Samantha was sitting right next to me and saw the same things. But why couldn't anyone else see them? Could it have been our glasses or maybe _____

_____

_____

_____

15. Thank goodness! I didn't eat it. The things it did to Jenny's face were awful. She looked like _____

_____

_____

_____

16. I must have been watching too many episodes of *Tales of the Unexplained*. It jumped right out at me. It looked like some alien being or a mutant of Jenny Rogers and Jimmy Johnson. Just as quickly as it arrived, it was gone. I started to wonder if I really did see it. It happened so fast. Then it came back bigger than before. Almost _____

_____

_____

_____

17. Food! Food! Food! I love food. Not just desserts, I am talking about all kinds of food. Yes, even spinach and liver. I can't think of a food that _____

_____

_____

_____

18. It is hard to describe how nice she really was. I miss her. Replacements are impossible to find _____

_____
_____
_____

19. Buy thermal! It will warm your heart and _____

_____
_____
_____

20. He surely was the most unforgettable character I ever met. I almost wished I was in school where my teacher would ask me to do a report on "An Unforgettable Character." He is so clear in my mind that it seems like yesterday when he _____

_____
_____
_____

21. These itches just won't go away. Camping trips are for the birds and bears, not people. They always build a bed of grass and leaves in my adventure books. This is an adventure just trying to stop from itching. My next camping trip will be different. It will _____

_____
_____
_____

22. My computer talks to me. It answers all my questions. It can think! There is no other computer like it. I am entering it in _____

_____
_____
_____

23. How many times can my horse throw me? Pretty soon everyone is going to realize I'm not from a ranch town in Texas. Why did I lie in the first place? Must have been that I didn't think they'd like me unless there was something really neat in my life. Another reason could have been that _____

_____
_____
_____

24. Hey! I like playing with dolls. There is no crime in playing with dolls. I find it very _____

_____
_____
_____

25. No one could catch the ball. It was a cross between a Mexican jumping bean and a kite. It was always just out of reach. It was only ten dollars, but _____

_____
_____
_____

26. Sarah was my best friend until that day we _____
_____
_____
_____

27. They told me that I wouldn't get another chance to qualify after today. I hope my best effort is good enough. I think I am ready. Only _____
_____
_____
_____

28. Ladies and Gentlemen! Welcome to Giovanni's sideshow of amazing humans and animals. You will see the two-headed woman, snake boy, the original spiderman, the fire-breathing baby and a group of exotic animals that includes _____
_____
_____
_____

29. Shoes, shoes, shoes! I can never find a pair that fits. Some people are just lucky. My feet are a size and a half different. That's not all that is different about me. Did you ever hear about a twelve-year-old that _____
_____
_____
_____
_____

30. The plane is almost out of gas. The runway is just ahead. Will we make it? Look out for the crosswind. Look to your left. It is going to _____
_____
_____
_____

31. There is something special about a good storyteller. They always have you sitting on the edge of your seat waiting for what is going to happen next. One minute you are laughing and the next you are sad. I remember how Mr. Tyler told that old tale about _____
_____
_____
_____

32. Looking out over the ocean from my favorite hillside has solved many of my problems. The ocean to me, like the country or meadows to others, seems to calm me down and let me see my problems a little more clearly. I remember the time I was really upset about
_____
_____
_____
_____

33. Just a stones throw away! They must have been kidding. I've been walking for miles. When I get there I am going to be years older. I almost forgot my mission. It is to rescue _____

_____

_____

34. The kite took right off. Little Billy couldn't let go. He was dragged into the sky the same way Little Ben was in the story "Ben and Me." The last thing I heard him say while he was being carried off was _____

_____

_____

35. This has been a raging battle in my family. Who is smarter, a dog or a turkey? My mother says that the dog is the smartest animal that ever lived. My dad says its the turkey, because the turkey _____

_____

_____

36. I'll boil the children just the way we witches are supposed to do it. A little garlic, a little spice, some cloves to make it nice. Then I'll wrap them and put them in the stew _____

_____

_____

37. Don't ever look under your bed at exactly twelve o'clock at night without these special beads around your neck. The last member of this family that looked _____

_____

_____

38. Most school buses stop at stop signs. This one went speeding through as if on a special mission to _____

_____

_____

39. This has really made me happy. It is a great present. What made you think I'd like _____

_____

_____

40. What is so special about the nutrients in Special Z cereal? You've come to the right person with your question. Take a look at my sister. She seems perfectly normal, doesn't she? Let me close the curtains and turn off the lights. Isn't that the most unique sight that you've ever seen? The only girl with _____

_____

_____

GA1329

41. Spelling is easy if you just remember these four simple rules _____

_____

_____

42. That now makes the one hundred and first time that Becky has beaten me at Monopoly. After the tenth time, I said I'd never play her again. But here I am, Mr. Loser once more. Surely she can't enjoy beating me that many times in a row. Yet, she yelled "yes" when I went belly up in the lose to her. I have tried every strategy that you can think of except

_____

_____

_____

43. Did you ever walk to school backwards? I am not talking about one block. I am talking about the whole way. It gives you a different picture of your neighborhood, school and friends. You see things like _____

_____

_____

44. Sand castles were my favorite type of architecture. They were never permanent. Yet, they always were a challenge. That challenge was, can you create something no one else had ever seen on a beach before. As you stand before my masterpiece, let me explain it to you. It represents _____

_____

_____

_____

45. I do not know which is worse, my dog or my sister following me to school. With one, I'm in trouble with the principal. With the other, I'm in trouble with Mom. It wasn't my fault when they both arrived at school on Thursday with their own playthings. Their playthings ran _____

_____

_____

46. Did you ever lose your smile in an apple? You know what that means? It's when _____

_____

_____

47. Cotton candy sticking to your face is better than all A's on your report card, a hug from Mom or even _____

_____

_____

158

48. Our bikes raced down the street neck and neck. This race was for bragging rights of the whole school. No one is going to ever call me Slowpoke again or tell my best friend that she is hanging out with a "training bike" expert. The finish line was in sight. Fifty yards to go. Then, "Oh, no _____

_____

_____

49. My lucky moon rock was doing strange things on my dresser with my lipstick. It just _____

_____

_____

50. Lemon water ice with real pieces of lemon in it is my favorite on a hot summer's night. It freezes your tongue, mouth and lungs if you eat it too quickly. That's what I like to do best. Eat it quickly. One night as I was gulping down an extra large one _____

_____

_____

_____

Ideas and Illustrations Supplement
Bulletin Boards

Dear cartographers, architects, sign painters, teachers, students and bulletin board makers of America,

There are ten pages in this section. Each page represents a month of the school year. The page is divided into two parts. The upper section contains an idea for a classroom or hall bulletin board for the particular month indicated. Teachers might want to take a piece of transparency paper, trace the bulletin board idea, put it on an overhead projector, and outline the enlarged image the projector creates. The lower section is a bulletin board that has been started but needs student help to complete. Students are asked to give their input as to the direction additional writing and illustration should take. Please complete the student bulletin board with your original and humorous ideas. A monthly clothesline of student bulletin boards makes a great display. A blank bulletin board has been provided below for students who would like to create a bulletin board from scratch. Students can use this blank board to create ideas for their other subjects as well. Transfer your best ideas to 11" x 14" (27.94 x 35.56 cm) art paper and pin the best work of the class up in the hallway. Try having a bulletin board contest after your teacher gives you a general theme for your original work.

Student name _____

My bulletin board theme is _____

GA1329

Bulletin Board Idea for September

Clear Your Mind for a Great Year

Student-Developed Bulletin Board for September

Starting the Dash for Great Books

GA1329

Bulletin Board Idea for October

Sliding into Children's Literature

Sliding into Children's Literature

350 FT.   CHARACTERS   350 FT.

OUTCOME   SETTING

PLOT

Student-Developed Bulletin Board for October

Let's Howl for a Good Book

Let's Howl for a Good Book

Bulletin Board Idea for November

Even the Headless Horseman Reads

Even the Headless Horseman Reads

RAMONA

Student-Developed Bulletin Board for November

Books Should Be Read, Not Pecked

Books Should Be Read, Not Pecked

GA1329

Bulletin Board Idea for December

Beverly Cleary Jingles Your Brain

Beverly Cleary Jingles Your Brain

Student-Developed Bulletin Board for December

Stormy Day Books

Stormy Day Books

GA1329

Bulletin Board Idea for January

Books Are Lifelong Friends

Student-Developed Bulletin Board for January

Three Pointers for Literature

Bulletin Board Idea for February

Heartbreaking Books for Sensitive Readers

Student-Developed Bulletin Board for February

These Books Deserve a Kiss

GA1329

Bulletin Board Idea for March
Books Build Bridges to Tomorrow

Student-Developed Bulletin Board for March
A Parade of Good Books

Bulletin Board Idea for April

Let These Books Put *Spring* into Your Step

Student-Developed Bulletin Board for April

Spring Fling Literature

Bulletin Board Idea for May

Sink Your Teeth into a Good Book

Student-Developed Bulletin Board for May

A Maypole of Good Ideas

GA1329

Bulletin Board Idea for June
Swim Over to a Good Book

Swim Over to a Good Book

A RAFT— ER OF BOOKS

Student-Developed Bulletin Board for June
Bury Your Head in a Book

Bury Your Head in a Book

170

GA1329

Answer Key

Vexing Vocabulary II, page 5

1. hazardous
2. silence
3. voice
4. jagged
5. checker
6. impatient
7. bur
8. margarine
9. guided
10. congregation

1. faucet
2. shivery
3. whetstones
4. tangled
5. Olympics
6. dainty
7. coziness
8. camera
9. moistened
10. conspicuous

Just the Facts, page 6

1. tomatoes
2. Picky-Picky
3. house payments, car payments, groceries and taxes
4. cheap cat food
5. in the dark in the church basement
6. The boys backed out at the last minute and their parts were filled by girls.
7. a couple/two
8. red
9. black
10. Ramona
11. He winked at her.
12. tail and headdress
13. as long as it wasn't complicated
14. tinsel
15. save money now that Dad lost job
16. Ramona's father
17. the jack-o'-lantern
18. burdock burs

Triple Play Words, page 12

1. snow
2. jumping
3. sea
4. ice
5. steam
6. hand
7. milk
8. some
9. merry
10. head
11. out
12. bed
13. house
14. bath
15. light
16. in
17. over
18. side
19. green
20. car

Just the Facts, page 20

1. her spelling
2. H and K
3. They both left messages in the front of the diary for the other one to "Keep Out."
4. *Ramona Quimby, Age 8*
5. a Chiquita banana sticker
6. Henry Huggins
7. She crushed it.
8. tin can
9. Pizzaface
10. panda
11. I's and T's
12. circles and figure eights
13. summer
14. Mrs. Whaley
15. Halloween
16. forty
17. very smart person

Just the Facts, page 37

1. Ribsy and Nosey
2. *Journal*
3. the dump
4. his mother
5. He could get his car in it, but he couldn't open the door of the car to get out in the garage.
6. an Indian and a wolf
7. a Dalmatian
8. TV commercials
9. a stuffed owl
10. A dog can have fleas, but fleas cannot have dogs.

11. She locked him in.
12. to buy a sleeping bag
13. Sheriff Bud

Just the Facts, page 50

1. second
2. Boyd
3. A-
4. his dad
5. a loner
6. retainers
7. Oregon
8. Albuquerque
9. poems and stories about horses
10. 6-volt lantern battery
11. medium
12. Wax Man
13. honorable mention
14. a nice man with a wicked twinkle in his eye
15. Leigh's mother

This Activity Is Old Hat or Brand-New, page 55

1. cold, ¼
2. knew, ¼
3. newt, ¼
4. Old Glory, ²⁄₈ = ¼
5. Newton, ²⁄₆ = ⅓
6. scold, ⅕
7. bold, ¼
8. Agnew, ⅖
9. fold, ¼
10. renewable, ⁴⁄₉
11. Old Maid, ³⁄₇
12. gold, ¼
13. brand new, ²⁄₈ = ¼
14. Old Faithful, ⁴⁄₁₁
15. mold, ¼

Vexing Vocabulary II, page 62

1. crib, 16
2. ribbon, 72
3. Caribbean, 243
4. caribou, 196
5. bribe, 125
6. cribbage, 384
7. tribe, 175
8. dribble, 392
9. horrible, 576
10. tributary, 810
11. tribute, 539
12. Tribune, 588

Just the Facts, page 63

1. fleas
2. shakes
3. tennis
4. diagonal
5. violets
6. column left
7. gnawing
8. kitchen
9. piano
10. fire escape
11. body and fender
12. collar free
13. loose
14. Pledge of Allegiance
15. asphalt

Inside Outs (Hard), page 67

1. entertain
2. effective
3. simulated
4. airplanes
5. carefully
6. geography
7. kilometer
8. incorrect
9. education
10. infuriate
11. escapades

Inside Outs (Easy), page 68

1. delighted
2. opposites
3. afterward
4. hamburger
5. important
6. whispered
7. tiptoeing
8. situation
9. struggles
10. stairwell
11. apartment
12. strenuous
13. telephone
14. fortunate
15. interrupt
16. shirttail

GA1329

Just the Facts, page 77

1. Sandra Norton's house
2. a boy
3. Sandra Norton's dog
4. permanent blue-black
5. Ogay otay eepslay.
6. chocolate Coke float/vanilla ice cream
7. an older crowd
8. next semester
9. a bamboo back-scratcher
10. George
11. Flavius
12. the rumble seat
13. a pun
14. Jane letting Buzz kiss her
15. Gladiolas

The World of Missing Spaces, page 82

1. Cleopatra
2. Nixon
3. Boone
4. Pitcher
5. Franklin
6. Revere
7. Tubman
8. Eisenhower
9. Truman
10. Lincoln
11. Columbus
12. Caesar
13. Hercules
14. Ross
15. Lindbergh
16. Earhart

1. stop, step
2. scroll, school
3. lily, tiny
4. clasp, flash
5. steam, steak
6. open, spin
7. grade, bride
8. allow, sloop

a. 2's
b. 11's
c. 3¾'s
d. 4¼'s
e. 12's
f. 20's
g. 13's
h. 9's

Critical and Creative Prefix Thinking, page 83

1. re
2. sub
3. in
4. mis
5. pre
6. con
7. im
8. com
9. non
10. anti
11. tri
12. mid

Vowel-itile Sentences, page 90

1. You can look but don't come too close.
2. He advanced, still hissing, through the rain.
3. Whoever heard of fresh kittens?
4. He was fascinated and frightened.
5. Are you sure exercise is perfect for the heart?
6. Who caused all the trouble, Socks or the little baby William?
7. We can't let a handsome boy get fat, can we?
8. No young upstart was going to tell him anything.
9. With his tail drooping, Ribsy looked around.
10. He did not have to mind his mother.

Just the Facts, page 91

1. Mrs. Risley
2. George/Debbie
3. station wagon
4. love
5. the typewriter
6. lap
7. the little girl next door
8. leftover formula
9. eight years old
10. Uncle Walts' bald head
11. salt free, low cholesterol
12. fifty
13. broom
14. Sitters' Service Agency
15. Scotch tape

Cat Got Your Tongue?, page 95

1. catsup, ²⁄₆ = ⅓
2. catastrophe, ⁴⁄₁₁
3. catch, ⅕
4. catacomb, ³⁄₈
5. scatter, ²⁄₇
6. Catholic, ³⁄₈
7. caterpillar, ⁴⁄₁₁
8. catalog, ³⁄₇
9. vacation, ½
10. vacant, ⅓
11. cathedral, ⅓
12. category, ³⁄₈
13. catapult, ³⁄₈
14. caterer, ²⁄₇
15. cattle, ⅓

Just the Facts, page 104

1. Vincente
2. velveteen
3. plow
4. mahogany
5. biology lab
6. cool things
7. talk to
8. fifty-three minutes
9. New Year's Eve
10. Mr. Ericson
11. Early American
12. roses
13. Jack
14. Jonas Hornbostle
15. Orange Belt
16. bard
17. the school newspaper
18. basketball
19. orange groves
20. airmail
21. Mr. Ericson's

Just the Facts, page 116

1. Mountain View Inn
2. grandfather
3. lonely
4. helmet
5. traps/poisons
6. eight
7. school
8. toothpaste
9. California
10. 1970's
11. Matt's pocket
12. beautiful mouse
13. by running a maze
14. Take me to the weeder.
15. Friday
16. Scotch tape
17. haiku
18. motorcycle was crushed

The Mice/Mouse Puzzle, page 122

1. grouse, 6 × 6 = 36
2. spices, 6 × 6 = 36
3. vice-president, 13 × 6 = 78
4. mouse/mice, 9 × 6 = 54
5. police, 6 × 6 = 36
6. slice, 5 × 6 = 30
7. housefly, 8 × 6 = 48
8. Venice, 6 × 6 = 36
9. juice, 5 × 6 = 30
10. trousers, 8 × 6 = 48
11. thrice, 6 × 6 = 36
12. mousse, 6 × 6 = 36
13. licorice, 8 × 6 = 48
14. price, 5 × 6 = 30
15. office, 6 × 6 = 36

Just the Facts, page 130

1. two years
2. six years
3. Cockroaches can't use capital key.
4. psychology
5. an alarm clock
6. thirteen
7. the bridal veil
8. apartment landlording
9. He didn't play basketball.
10. character
11. Latin
12. fifty years
13. Robin
14. Plato: Teacher and Theorist
15. shirt
16. a Vespa motor scooter
17. guitar
18. an innocent kiss
19. Praetorian
20. laurel
21. dish towels
22. Giants and Dodgers

Just the Facts, page 142

1. five
2. Valerie
3. *The Pied Piper*
4. Mrs. Gitler
5. She was too plump.
6. three feet
7. a riding academy
8. science
9. an old tire pump
10. monkeys/trees

GA1329